JAPAN AT THE POLLS

JAPAN AT THE POLLS

The House of Councillors
Election of 1974

Edited by Michael K. Blaker

American Enterprise Institute for Public Policy Research
Washington, D. C.

JQ1694
J38

ISBN 0-8447-3213-3

Foreign Affairs Study 37, August 1976

Library of Congress Catalog Card No. 76-023589

Printed in the United States of America

CONTENTS

EDITOR'S NOTE

Japanese Names

In the essays in this study Japanese names are cited in accordance with conventional Japanese usage, that is, family name first and given name last.

Abbreviations

For the sake of convenience, the names of the Japanese political parties have been abbreviated as follows:

> LDP—Liberal Democratic party (Jiyū Minshutō)
> JSP—Japan Socialist party (Nihon Shakaitō)
> KMT—Clean Government party (Kōmeitō)
> JCP—Japan Communist party (Nihon Kyōsantō)
> DSP—Democratic Socialist party (Minshatō)

Crossreferencing

To avoid repetition and to make the study a coherent whole, the statistical data and (where appropriate) the interpretative material in the papers have been crossreferenced in the footnotes.

Statistical Data

For purposes of consistency, calculations are based upon or checked against data contained in Shakai Chōsa Kenkyūsho [Marketing Intelligence Corporation] and Nihon Seiji Sōgō Kenkyūsho [The Institute for Political Studies in Japan], eds., *Sangiin senkyo—shiryō to bunseki—1974* [Japanese upper house election—1974] (Tokyo: Shakai Chōsa Kenkyūsho, 1974). Where source references are not given in the text or the Appendix, the reader may assume that the data are available in this volume.

PREFACE

This analysis of the 1974 House of Councillors election in Japan is one of a series of studies of national elections in parliamentary democracies being undertaken by the American Enterprise Institute for Public Policy Research (AEI). Other volumes in the AEI series cover the 1974 British parliamentary elections, the presidential election in France, and the general election in Canada.

This study deals with a Japanese national election of great political importance. For over a year Japanese political observers had looked ahead to 1974 as the year of the House of Councillors election, a political watershed for Prime Minister Tanaka Kakuei and his ruling Liberal Democratic party (LDP). Declining public support for the LDP, hastened by the jarring impact of the energy crisis on the Japanese economy, convinced many people that a conservative defeat was possible. A loss for the LDP in the election would endanger the party's slender majority in the 252-member upper chamber. Beyond that, it was claimed that if the opposition should gain control of the Councillors, LDP prospects for the 1975 local and general elections and Tanaka's own political fate would hang in the balance.

At stake in Japan's tenth triennial House of Councillors election were 130 seats[1]—54 to be filled from a list of 112 candidates in a nationwide contest (called unaffectionately by some the All-Japan Derby) and 76 from 237 candidates running in 47 local prefectural constituencies which elect from 1 to 4 members each. Despite the prophecies of impending LDP disaster during the winter of 1973, as the election approached the forecasts pointed to an LDP victory of modest proportions (70–75 seats). But in a dramatic surprise, the LDP

---

[1] Half the seats are contested every three years, and in 1974 there were an additional four vacancies.

won just 62 seats, far fewer than virtually everyone had predicted. The LDP was left clinging precariously to a 7-seat majority in the Councillors. Also, the reports of widespread corruption and bribery during the campaign, particularly directed against LDP candidates, badly tarnished Tanaka's personal reputation and helped bring about the resignation of two top cabinet members in a swirl of postelection controversy over campaign ethics and party reform. Aside from the new distribution of seats in the Councillors, which many thought would cause legislative paralysis, it was the political tremors affecting the Tanaka prime ministership and domestic Japanese political stability that made the 1974 election of such consequence.

The three essays in this study are intended to place the 1974 election against the backdrop of ongoing patterns of institutional, political, and social change in contemporary Japan. In the first paper, Herbert Passin traces several major themes in the historical evolution of the House of Councillors system, beginning with an overview of the Councillors' predecessor, the prewar House of Peers. He identifies the main expectations that the Japanese and American Occupation architects had for the postwar upper house: it would perform a checking or balancing function vis-à-vis the lower house, it would represent "national" over more parochial local interests, it would give a legislative voice to special interest groups and other organizations, and it would help maintain political equilibrium in the face of possible excesses of public opinion and political partisanship. Passin then contrasts these expectations with the system that has developed, describing the politicization of the House of Councillors and its constitutional weakness relative to the lower house. Nevertheless Passin concludes that the House of Councillors has managed to retain a separate institutional identity and has provided for the representation of segments of Japanese society, including some of the weaker political groupings, that might otherwise have been excluded from the governmental process.

One of the aspects of the 1974 Councillors election that distinguished it from past Japanese national elections was the extent of public concern with the conduct of the campaign itself, especially the commitment of the financial and organizational resources of some of Japan's biggest corporations to the campaigns of individual candidates. In the second essay of this study, Gerald Curtis deals with the election campaign and provides details, many of which come from his own observations and experience, of what many observers thought was the dirtiest and most expensive campaign in postwar Japanese politics. He describes the imprint of Tanaka and top conservative leaders on the LDP campaign, as the ruling conservatives tried to return to the more familiar ground of ideological bipolarity that characterized Japanese politics in the 1950s and 1960s. Curtis also explores another dimension of the election—the relationship between the institutional structure and the political process—specifically, the process by which the political structure affects voting behavior and the campaign strategies of the various political parties. He argues that interparty competition in Japan is growing and intensifying and, with the spread of urbanization, the result may be a multiparty system of the type now encountered only in the multimember metropolitan districts.

The third essay, by the editor of this volume, is primarily concerned with the aggregate data of the 1974 election and the impact of several key variables—most notably urbanization—upon political support structures and political party performance. For a variety of reasons, party support structures in labor, agriculture, and business appear to be weakening. The July 1974 election was a political index of some of the significant changes that have been taking place in the nature and composition of the Japanese electorate. Partly as a result of these changes, party support has declined and the number of uncommitted voters has risen. It is also evident that the various parties, painfully aware of their weakening popularity, were eager to devise ways of expanding their appeal into other segments of the population. The 1974 election suggests that the degree of fragmentation and loosening of party support structures has been exaggerated, particularly by the media. Nonetheless, the balance of political forces in Japan is more fluid than ever before, a fact that has serious implications for the future direction of Japanese politics.

Support from AEI enabled the authors to spend the 1974 election period in Japan, where they had the opportunity to observe developments first-hand and to talk with journalists, politicians, and scholars about events as they unfolded. One of the scholars was Tomita Nobuo, who has written extensively on subjects relating to Japanese politics and electoral behavior. His articles on the 1971 House of Councillors election are the most comprehensive and reliable studies available. For this study Tomita assembled many useful statistical data on the 1974 election, and these are included in the Appendix.

Considerable time has passed since the 1974 House of Councillors election, but there is still no consensus on the contours of the emerging political order in Japan. Nor is there unanimity about the exact meaning of the 1974 election for the future of Japanese political development. For example, the reader will find slight differences of opinion and interpretation among the three authors in this study. While the unpredictable nature of Japanese politics makes generalizing a risky business, it is hoped that these essays, along with the statistical information provided, will give those interested in Japanese politics an idea of the strength, vibrancy, and complexity of the contemporary Japanese democratic process.

MICHAEL K. BLAKER

1

THE HOUSE OF COUNCILLORS: PROMISE AND ACHIEVEMENT

Herbert Passin

Origins

In 1947 the American Occupation authorities described with quiet satisfaction a major achievement, the new House of Councillors (Sangiin), the upper house of the bicameral legislature established after the war. It was, they said, a "unique and perhaps revolutionary method of dual-constituency selection."[1] Unlike its predecessor, the prewar House of Peers (Kizokuin),[2] the new body was to be entirely elected. Unlike most elected bodies, however, it had two different kinds of constituency. The local constituency (*chihōku*), from which 152 of its 252 members are elected, is in principle no different from the constituencies of the more familiar geographically based representation system of the lower house, except that the electoral districts are much larger. Instead of being divided into several districts, each prefecture constitutes a single district. But the national constituency (*zenkokku*) is indeed unique. Its 100 members are chosen from the country at large in an election by single-entry ballot, a kind of national popularity contest in which everyone has one vote. The term of office for both the local and national members is six years,[3] and one-half of the members are rotated every three years.

---

[1] Supreme Commander for the Allied Powers (SCAP), General Headquarters (GHQ): *Political Reorientation of Japan—September 1945 to September 1948*, vol. 1 (Washington, D.C.: U.S. Government Printing Office, 1949), p. 185 (hereafter cited as *Political Reorientation*).

[2] The House of Peers in prewar Japan was part hereditary, part appointed, and part elected from highly specialized constituencies.

[3] With two exceptions: the first election in 1947 when all (at that time) 250 members had to be elected at once, and by-elections for seats that fall vacant, which have a three-year term.

This unusual system carries all the earmarks of the compromise it represents between the prewar House of Peers and the American Occupation's original desire for a unicameral assembly. The Occupation has often been criticized for mechanically imposing American-style reforms on Japanese institutions. Whatever may be the case in other fields, this complaint is not justified here. In spite of the fact that the American legislature is bicameral, the Occupation originally favored a unicameral system for Japan. It was the Japanese side that wanted some form of upper house. What eventually took shape emerged from the dialectic of these two very different positions.

A brief consideration of the prewar House of Peers, from which the House of Councillors system developed, may be useful in understanding how the present system came about.

The House of Peers, 1890–1947. The Japanese parliament, or Diet,[4] came into existence in November 1890. Under the Meiji constitution, promulgated on 11 February 1889 (Article 33), an "Imperial Diet" (Teikoku Gikai) was to be established, constituted of two chambers: a House of Representatives (Shūgiin), elected by the people, and a House of Peers (Kizokuin), composed of "the members of the Imperial Family, of the orders of nobility, and of those persons who have been nominated thereto by the Emperor" (Article 34). The ordinance governing the composition of the House of Peers was promulgated on the same day as the constitution itself.

The first House of Peers, that of 1890, started out with 252 members (curiously, exactly the same number as the present House of Councillors), but later moved up to an average of somewhat over 400. Six classes of members were defined: (1) princes of the blood, (2) non-Imperial princes (kōshaku) and marquises (kōshaku),[5] (3) counts (hakushaku), viscounts (shishaku), and barons (danshaku), (4) Imperial appointees, named for meritorious achievement, public contribution, or service to the state, (5) representatives of the highest taxpayers in each prefecture, and (6) members of the Imperial Academy. Imperial princes automatically became life members at eighteen. Nonimperial princes and marquises became life members at thirty. Imperial appointees and members of the Imperial Academy held their

---

[4] The use of this German term as a translation for the name of the national legislature was initiated by the Meiji government authorities, anxious to stress the Germanic (as against the English) inspiration. Since then, this usage has become universal in European languages.

[5] Although the words for these two types of kōshaku are pronounced the same, they are written with different Chinese characters and are two different words.

membership for seven-year terms, unless reappointed. The lower-nobility members were elected by their respective orders for seven-year terms. The highest-taxpayer members, who had to be forty years of age or older, were elected by the fifteen highest taxpayers in their respective prefectures for seven-year terms.

Under the Meiji constitution the Diet as a whole had powers severely restricted in comparison with those of the other elements of government, such as the Throne, the Privy Council, the Council of Elders (Genrōin), and the Cabinet. But whatever the extent of the Diet's authority under the constitution, both houses were to be equal in principle. In reality, however, the House of Peers had very considerable powers that frequently gave it an edge over the House of Representatives in the legislative process.

The superiority of the Peers was symbolically shown in the fact that appearances of the Emperor before the Diet always took place in the Peers' chamber with the president of the Peers presiding. Moreover, while almost all of the members of the Peers held titles of nobility or high court rank, the members of the Representatives held court rank somewhat below that of bureau chiefs in the bureaucracy. Very few bills originated in the lower house, and those that passed the lower house usually died in the Peers, either through formal rejection or mere inaction—which had the same effect, since no bills could be carried over from one session to the next.

By and large, then, the House of Peers acted as a conservative counterweight to the popularly elected Representatives, usually supporting authority, conservative measures, and the government. But the Peers on a number of occasions voted down a government budget or part of it. In 1901, for example, a majority of the members of the Peers supported Field-Marshal Prince Yamagata Aritomo and voted down the budget of Prime Minister Itō Hirobumi. It required an Imperial rescript to force them to change their minds. On several other occasions, as in 1893 and 1914, they introduced crippling amendments to government military budgets that forced the government to take extraordinary measures. In 1893, it took an Imperial rescript offering to contribute 10 percent from the civil list to force the Peers to back down. In 1914, the Peers' elimination of 70 million yen from the naval appropriations bill helped bring down the Yamamoto cabinet. In the 1920s and 1930s, the House of Peers repeatedly acted against the government in power, usually siding with the conservative Privy Council. Because of its objection to some wording in the Kellogg-Briand antiwar pact signed by the government of Tanaka Giichi—and later repudiated by the government under

3

pressure—the Peers killed a number of important government bills. In 1930, because of its opposition to the London Naval Treaty, the Peers threatened to hold up the entire legislative program of the Hamaguchi government. But despite occasional assertions of independence, the House of Peers was a pillar of conservative rule and, in the view of many Japanese liberals, a major obstacle to democratic development in the prewar period.

The Japanese and American Proposals. To the American Occupation a House of Peers was by definition undemocratic. The democratization program called for the abolition of the peerage system, naturally leaving no place for a House of Peers. At the request of the Occupation authorities, Prime Minister Shidehara Kijūrō appointed a Constitution Problems Study Committee (Kenpō Mondai Chōsa Iinkai) in October 1945. Its chairman was State Minister Matsumoto Jōji. It is clear that in considering the character of the legislature to be established under the new constitution, Matsumoto thought of the upper house as a slightly reformed House of Peers; he preferred a house with both elected and appointed members but he was willing, if necessary, to give up the peerage members.

The study committee examined many alternative ways of selecting upper house members. These included proportional representation; functional or occupational representation; majority or plurality election from House of Representatives districts; indirect election by local authorities, such as prefectural or city assemblies; appointment of some members and election of others; election by the House of Representatives; and election by the cabinet. As late as January 1946, the Matsumoto draft, then being deliberated by the committee, stated, "The House of Councillors shall be composed of members elected publicly, or appointed by the Emperor, according to occupational fields, geographical areas, and learning and experience, as provided for by law"; [6] even the critics of this draft called for election by "local deliberative assemblies" of "members who are the representatives of various occupations." [7]

Occupation thinking was on an entirely different track. It regarded direct election as essential to the democratic character of the legislature, a concept that was to be embodied in Article 53 of the new constitution ("Both Houses shall consist of elected members, representatives of all the people"). When Matsumoto and other members of the committee met with the Occupation's Government

---

[6] *Political Reorientation*, vol. 2, p. 608.

[7] Ibid., p. 613 (draft submitted around 1 February 1946).

Section in mid-February 1946, they were shocked to discover that the Occupation favored a unicameral system. The Government Section's draft constitution stated that "the Diet shall consist of one House of elected representatives with a membership of not less than 300 nor more than 500."[8] There is "no need for a House of Peers because the peerage is abolished . . . no need for establishing the concept of dual representation of state sovereignties and the people as in the United States."[9] Matsumoto, stunned by this proposal, argued with Government Section's General Courtney Whitney that a single house was "so completely foreign to the historic development of the Japanese legislative body that he wondered what thoughts had actuated this provision," to which Whitney replied that in view of the abolition of the peerage and the absence of regional sovereignties, "a single house was simplest."[10] But although the Americans would have preferred a single house, they were prepared to yield if the Japanese felt strongly about a bicameral legislature since the new upper house, whatever its shape, was bound to be the weaker of the two. They also foresaw that they might use the issue as a bargaining counter.

The Occupation had specified three principles: direct popular election, equal representation, and equal qualifications for the electors for the two houses. This presented the Japanese with the problem of how to make the two houses different if both had to be elected by direct popular vote. The solution was found in three devices. First, although the qualifications of voters for the two houses had to be the same, the Occupation was willing to accept differences in the qualifications of the members of the two houses. Accordingly, the lower age limit for House of Representatives' members was set at twenty-five, but that for the House of Councillors at thirty. Second, to meet the requirement of equal representation, geographically defined electoral districts had to be established. For these the analogy of the statewide district of the U.S. Senate strongly suggested the prefecture as the base: at the time, the United States had forty-eight states and Japan had forty-six (if Okinawa were counted, forty-seven) prefectures. But while this arrangement was expected to produce legislators somewhat different from those elected in the smaller districts of the lower house, it would not produce those unique features of the House of Peers system that the framers wished to retain: the presence

[8] Takayanagi Kenzō, Ōtomo Ichirō, and Tanaka Hideo, *Nihonkoku kenpō seitei no katei* (Tokyo: Yuhikaku, 1952), vol. 1, p. 282. Draft dated 13 February 1946.
[9] Ibid., p. 310.
[10] Ibid., pp. 330-332.

of distinguished national personages, scholars, writers, scientists, nonpoliticians, devoted to the national rather than the party or provincial interest, and representatives of diffuse constituencies. To achieve this a third approach was proposed: direct election from prefectural electoral districts as well as Imperial appointment, or appointment by the lower house, or national elections for candidates nominated by the lower house. All of these were rejected as inconsistent with the Occupation's requirements and with the constitution. If this national constituency were not to be achieved by Imperial appointment or by some other nonrepresentative device, then it had to be achieved by direct elections. Thus, the dual-constituency system of the upper house came into being. It was assumed that the age difference between the members of the two houses, even though slight, when coupled with differences in the nature of the electoral districts, would make it possible for the upper house to develop a distinctive character.

The discussions continued through 1946. The final draft was submitted to the Diet in November 1946, passed by the House of Peers on 25 December 1946, and then, upon passing the lower house, became law. When the House of Councillors law was promulgated on 24 February 1947, the House of Peers ceased to exist. The first House of Councillors was elected on 20 April 1947.

Expectations. What expectations did the framers of the House of Councillors hold with regard to its function in a democratic Japanese polity? It is quite clear that the Japanese hoped to retain as many as possible of the features they saw as desirable in the old House of Peers system. Of these, four were salient.

First and foremost, an upper house was considered essential to a system of checks and balances. The popularly elected House of Representatives was not to be fully trusted. As Matsumoto explained to General Whitney—echoing, perhaps unconsciously, the American founding fathers' arguing the need for a Senate as a check on the House of Representatives [11]—"If only one house existed . . . one party will get a majority and go to an extreme and then another party will come in and go to the opposite extreme. . . ." [12] Upper house members, it was believed, would be nonpartisan, sage, judicious, experienced—in a sense, above the battle. The upper house could check hasty or ill-considered actions of the lower house and would review bills prepared by the lower house. It could delay their passage long enough to assure full discussion and the expression of public opinion,

[11] See the *Federalist*, no. 62 and no. 63.
[12] Takayanagi, Ōtomo, and Tanaka, *Nihonkoku kenpō*, p. 332.

and it was expected that the upper house could play a stabilizing role in the event that the lower house were split over some issue along partisan lines.

Second, it was expected that the upper house would represent the larger national interest as against the parochial local interests represented by the members of the House of Representatives. This was widely regarded as one of the advantages of the House of Peers that should be retained. That system—representation by the "best elements" of the nation—had ensured that the wider national interests would always be kept in mind, counterweight to the shortsighted passions of the people's representatives. Since the House of Councillors, unlike the House of Peers, was to be elected, however, the framers were challenged to create an electoral system capable of yielding the desired result. The larger constituencies designed for the upper house were one means: instead of the 123 districts that elected representatives, there were only 46 districts (since the return of Okinawa to Japan in 1972, 47) for the upper house, one for each prefecture. But what was expected to come closest to achieving the national representativeness of the old House of Peers was the national-constituency system. Those elected in this constituency would need far more than purely local appeal.

Third, the bicameral system was regarded as a form of proportional representation. An upper house would provide for representation of elements unlike those that would be elected through the lower house electoral system. As in the old House of Peers, but this time by election, there would be intellectuals, distinguished public figures, and nonprofessionals of all kinds representing a diversity of interests and points of view. In small electoral districts men of this caliber might not be elected; they would need a larger arena in which to mobilize their strength. Many distinguished persons whom it would be desirable to have in the deliberative councils of state might be reluctant to submit themselves to the demeaning requirements of local politics. Larger constituencies would tend to bring forth nationally known figures as well as prominent local men. Persons elected from the larger constituencies, it was expected, would be different in character from the usual politicians of the lower body, and very likely superior. Without this more dignified type of upper house, the services of such men might be lost to the nation.

A further expectation was that the upper house would allow representation for diverse functional or occupational interest groups. An upper house, particularly if some members were elected by a national constituency, would provide an opportunity for the representation of diffuse constituencies that were not sufficiently concentrated in any single electoral district to gain election, such as religious groups, interest groups, labor unions, farm organizations, and professional associations. In the deliberations on the Japanese side the necessity of some kind of occupational or functional representation was a constant refrain. Members of the Constitution Problems Study Committee kept coming back to one or another variant of this idea; the Japan Socialist party even took the position that the House of Councillors should be elected by functional and occupational organizations. Since the Americans rejected this position as inconsistent with the principle of direct election by the people, the national-constituency idea appeared all the more attractive as a means of achieving this end.

Fourth, as the founding fathers had said about the American Senate, an upper house could provide stability and continuity. Since the composition of the lower house would be wedded to the exigencies of party politics, it would change frequently. A second house with an independent—and longer—term of office would be the balance wheel of government. It would, as Matsumoto maintained at his meeting with General Whitney on 13 February 1946, give stability to the operation of the legislature and to the policies of government.

Checks and Balances

How did these expectations—or hopes—fare? By 1974, when the tenth triennial elections were held, the House of Councillors had been in existence for twenty-seven years, time enough perhaps to see how the system has worked out.

The first of the framers' expectations—that the House of Councillors would serve as a check on excessive or improper actions of the lower house—presupposes the fulfillment of several conditions. The upper house must first have the power to do so. And having the power, it must have the will to exercise it, which means that it must have some independence. Independence rests not only on the formal rules governing the relations of the two houses but also on the extent to which the upper house is nonpartisan, or at least different in the distribution of its political affiliations from the lower house.

The Power of the House. The prewar House of Peers had the power to veto many actions of the lower house. But the Occupation authorities were determined to prevent domination by the upper house in the postwar legislature. If there were to be a bicameral Diet, then they favored one along the lines of the British system, in which the House of Commons has the real power, rather than one like the American Congress, where the Senate has superior power.

Japan's postwar constitution gives the lower house dominance in several critical respects. First, when the two houses disagree over a bill, the House of Councillors can be overridden by a two-thirds vote of the lower house (Article 59). Second, the budget must first be submitted to the lower house; then, if the House of Councillors "makes a decision different from that of the House of Representatives . . . or in the case of failure by the House of Councillors to take final action within thirty days . . . the decision of the House of Representatives shall be the decision of the Diet" (Article 60). On the budget, then, the Councillors can delay an action only for thirty days.[13] Third, in case of disagreement over treaties, the lower house prevails (Article 61); in the American Congress, on the contrary, it is the Senate that must ratify treaties. Fourth, when the houses disagree over the election of the prime minister or when the House of Councillors fails to act within ten days after the Representatives have designated their choice, the decision of the Representatives prevails (Article 67). Fifth, if the House of Representatives is dissolved, the House of Councillors is automatically prorogued. It is not, however, dissolved.

The main, although to date purely theoretical, area of superiority of the Councillors arises from this last consideration. In an emergency, when the lower house is in a state of dissolution, the cabinet is constitutionally empowered to convoke an emergency session of the House of Councillors. However, unless the House of Representatives agrees to upper house actions taken in such an emergency session within ten days of the opening of the next Diet session, they become null and void (Article 54).

The Councillors' inferior constitutional position is further reflected in its generally subordinate status in the political process. The prime ministership and most—and certainly the most important— cabinet posts and parliamentary vice-ministerships go to lower house members. Only one major party post is allocated to the upper house.

Since 1956 an informal quota of two or three cabinet posts for members of the House of Councillors has been in operation. In the first Tanaka cabinet, formed in 1972, three of the twenty-one cabinet posts—Transport, Science and Technology, and Defense—were held by councillors, as were six of the twenty-four parliamentary vice-ministerships; in the third, formed in November 1974, councillors

---

[13] Excluding recess periods during that time.

held two cabinet positions—Transport, and Posts and Telecommunications. The Miki cabinet, formed in December 1974, gave three posts to councillors (Transport, the Director of the Prime Minister's Office, and the Okinawa Development Agency),[14] and seven of the twenty-five parliamentary vice-ministerships also went to councillors.[15] (Each ministry has an administrative vice-minister [*jimu jikan*], who is a civil servant, and at least one parliamentary vice-minister [*seimu jikan*], who is a member of the Diet.)

But even though cabinet posts might seem to be a gauge of the Councillors' political weight, there are many, including some councillors, who believe that cabinet posts are a form of cooptation. By accepting ministerial office, a councillor shares responsibility for government policy and surrenders the independent, nonpartisan role of critic originally envisioned for the Councillors. Since he is taken into the cabinet largely as a representative of his party faction, the other members of his faction are also implicated and therefore disarmed as critics.

Because of the Councillors' weak position, ambitious politicians usually run for the lower house rather than for the Councillors. A not uncommon pattern is for senior civil servants to stand for their first election in the national constituency, where their national organizational connections can be brought to bear, and then, after having established themselves and acquired some parliamentary experience and reputation, to run in the far stiffer competition for lower house seats. This was the path followed by Miyazawa Kiichi, foreign minister in the Miki cabinet, who, after a career as a top civil servant, entered politics in 1953 as a House of Councillors candidate in Hiroshima Prefecture. After winning and serving two terms there, he then ran as a candidate for the House of Representatives from Hiroshima's Third District, from which he has since been continuously reelected. Aichi Kiichi, foreign minister in the Satō cabinet, also crossed from the civil service to politics via the House of Councillors, where he served one term before entering the rough-and-tumble of lower house politics. When the famous writer, Ishihara Shintarō— elected to the Councillors in 1968 with an unprecedented 3 million votes—decided to throw himself more deeply into politics, he resigned

---

[14] The post of education minister was given to a nonpolitician, sociologist Nagai Michio, a move virtually unprecedented since the 1950s.

[15] The first Tanaka cabinet had twenty-one cabinet posts (ministries, agencies, and offices) and twenty-four parliamentary vice-ministerships. The Miki cabinet has one additional cabinet position, the National Land Development Agency, but since some members hold more than one portfolio, there are only twenty ministers (in addition to the prime minister).

from the upper house and ran for the lower house in the tough Tokyo Second District (where he also finished in first place).

While several dozen former councillors have moved to the greener pastures of the lower house, about thirty of the present councillors began their political careers in the lower house. If those who move from the Councillors to the Representatives are in search of more action, perhaps those who go the other way are seeking the less demanding political life of the upper house.

Independence. Formally, the House of Councillors is free to conduct its activities without lower house or cabinet interference. The House of Councillors has its own committee system, which differs somewhat from that of the lower house, and a slightly distinctive deliberative process. Unlike the speaker of the lower house, the Councillors' speaker is nonpartisan. He casts a vote only in the event of a tie on the floor of the House. This situation has developed since 1971 when Kōno Kenzō, elected as a Liberal-Democrat, ran for the speakership against the party-designated candidate, Kiuchi Shiho. For the first time party discipline failed to hold: there was a "revolt," and Kōno, with the support of dissident Liberal Democratic party and opposition members, won out over the official LDP candidate. He then resigned from the LDP and therewith established the precedent of speakers being nonpartisan, even if they must resign from their party to be so.

In practice, however, independence depends upon the extent to which members are controlled by their party. If all members are subject to the control of one party or another, then the upper house becomes a rubber stamp for the actions of the lower house. The framers of the House of Councillors system had wanted to prevent this from happening. If the upper house were to perform its proper function of restraining the excesses of the lower house or supplementing its deficiencies, its members would have to be independent, exercise individual judgment, and avoid the party discipline of the lower house. What led Kōno to take the action that he did was his view, articulated in the 1960s, that the upper house should be a place where party control is not tightly exercised.[16]

These are some of the virtues of the old House of Peers that the Japanese desired to retain in the Councillors. However, despite its appointive character and its reputation as the bastion of opposition to party government, the old House of Peers was not entirely immune from partisanship. There were factions within the Peers, the most

---

[16] Tsuji Kiyoaki, ed., *Shiryō—sengo 20-nenshi*, vol. 1 (Tokyo: Nihon Hyōron Sha, 1966), p. 210.

important of which was the Kenkyūkai or "Research Association." After World War I, and particularly following the outbreak of the Manchurian Incident in 1931, the political parties succeeded in making some inroads among the Peers.

The Decline of the Independents. When the results of the first House of Councillors election in 1947 came in, it looked as if the system were indeed working as the framers had hoped. Of the 250 seats at stake, independents had won 111—a majority (57) of the 100 national seats and 54 of the 150 local seats. (The remaining 139 seats were distributed as follows: the JSP—47, the Liberals [Jiyutō, one of the two main conservative parties]—38, the Democratic party (Minshutō, the other main conservative party)—28, the Japan Communist party—4, and other parties—22.)

Even more exciting was the fact that many of those elected in the national constituency, and particularly the independents, were men of distinction of precisely the kind that had been hoped for: scholars, writers, national leaders, and representatives of specialized constituencies. One of the highest vote-getters in the national constituency was Socialist Matsumoto Jiichirō, the representative of the *burakumin* (former untouchables), who, because of his large vote, was elected vice-speaker of the House of Councillors.

Within a month of the election the spirit of independence came to be embodied in the newly formed Ryokufūkai, the Green Breeze Society, given its name by the writer Yamamoto Yūzō, himself elected in the national constituency. The Ryokufūkai set out to bring together nonparty independents and even a few independent spirits among party members (such as Wada Hirō of the JSP). The first seventy-seven members included scholars such as Takase Sōtarō and Tanaka Kōtarō;[17] writers and cultural figures such as Yamamoto and Hani Gorō; representatives of religious organizations; the first three speakers of the House; Fujii Heigo, vice-president of the Yawata Steel Corporation; and many other distinguished personages. The following month, with the admission of members of the small National Cooperative party (Kokumin Kyōdōtō) and the Independents Club (Mushozoku Kurabu), the membership of the Ryokufūkai reached its high point, ninety-six. This loose association, whose members were unaffiliated with any political party, had become the largest grouping in the upper house.

---

[17] Tanaka had been a distinguished professor of law at Tokyo University and was later minister of education, chief justice of the Supreme Court, and finally justice on the Permanent Court of International Justice of the League of Nations.

The Ryokufūkai sought to represent the ideal spirit of the upper house: independence and the national "constituency of good sense" (*ryōshiki no fu*). No strict rules were formulated and members were free to act in accordance with their own views. But this brave spirit of independence very soon began to give way to party control. The decline of the Ryokufūkai and the growing politicization of the Councillors may be seen in the fact that the number of Ryokufūkai declined from ninety-six in 1947 to fifty-seven in 1950, to forty-eight in 1953, to twenty-nine in 1956, to eleven in both 1959 and 1962, thence to four in 1965, and none in 1968.[18]

Contrast the situation after the 1974 elections with that after the first elections of 1947. In 1947, 111 independents had been elected, obtaining 59 percent of the vote in the national constituency and 34 percent in the local constituencies. The largest grouping in the House was the Ryokufūkai. By 1974, however, there were only 8 independents left (including those elected from minor parties). In the 1974 election, independents won 13 percent of the national and 5 percent of the local-constituency votes and several of them affiliated with parties immediately after the election.

If the Ryokufūkai is taken as an index of upper house independence, then it is clear that this independence began to decline right after its great triumph in the first House of Councillors election. In the second election in June 1950, nineteen of the incumbent independents lost their seats and, with the defection of others to the government party, only fifty-seven were left in the Ryokufūkai. With this, the Ryokufūkai dropped from first to third place among groups in the Councillors, overtaken by the Liberal party (seventy-seven seats) and the JSP (sixty-two seats). From then on its decline was steady.

The turning point came in 1956, when Ryokufūkai membership dropped to twenty-nine. In 1955 Japanese politics began to move toward what many people hailed as a two-party system. The JSP, which had split into left and right wings in 1953, united and, partially in self-protection, the conservatives brought their principal factions together in late 1955 to form the Liberal Democratic party. The two united parties had much stronger appeal both to the electorate and to the elected Councillors than did the fragmented parties.

The decline of the independents, however, was not only due to the sudden attractiveness of the two large parties. It also came about because, in order to attain high post, whether in the cabinet, as a

---

[18] In 1960 the Ryokufūkai renamed itself the Dōshikai or "Comrades Association."

13

parliamentary vice-minister, or as chairman of a House committee, one had to belong to the government party. From the very start of the House of Councillors system, therefore, there was a steady attrition of independents attracted by the lure of high position. Since the Ryokufūkai had no disciplinary powers over its members, it could not prevent their accepting cabinet or other desirable posts. Little by little, independents succumbed to the blandishments of the government party.

But perhaps the single key factor in the Ryokufūkai's decline was the need for party support in elections. In the national constituency, a candidate today needs at least 550,000 votes to win. Yet it would be physically impossible—quite apart from the enormous costs involved—for a candidate to get around all, or even a significant part, of the country in the twenty-five days originally allotted for the election campaign. (The campaign has since been shortened to twenty-three days.) Without organized support reaching into the towns and villages, a candidate cannot secure the hundreds of thousands of votes he needs. Even if he tries to mobilize most of his votes from only one or two prefectures, he still needs organized support. The most successful of these candidates have been from parties with effective organizational structures, Kōmeitō and the JCP. In the 1974 election, Miki Tadao, a KMT incumbent, took 85 percent of his national votes in Tokyo; the 684,000 Tokyo votes alone were enough to elect him. Komaki Toshio, chairman of the Executive Committee of the Osaka High School Teachers Union, running for his first term on the JCP ticket, won 81 percent of his votes in his home district of Osaka; since this still left him over 100,000 short, it was the scattered remainder of his votes that gave him his seat. He finished in 50th place. Independent Ichikawa Fusae, who came in second, was an exception. Without organizational support, her young irregulars won her almost all the votes she needed from Tokyo, even though this represented only 29 percent of her very large vote; the Tokyo vote together with her votes from neighboring Kanagawa Prefecture gave her all she needed. The system gives the advantage to candidates with nation-wide reputations and those with the support of national organizations such as trade unions, professional associations, and religious bodies. Others need party support.

In the local constituencies as well, the need for organized support has turned candidates toward the parties and undermined their independence. The prefecture-wide local constituency, although obviously much more easily coverable than the national, is usually much larger than the electoral districts of the lower house. Each of the local constituencies has within it lower house districts controlled by lower house members whose support structures, connections, and roots are there. The upper house prefectural-constituency candidate, needing their support to win, is more likely to compromise his independence than the national-constituency candidate. While in the national constituency it is possible for nationally known celebrities and representatives of national organizations to win as independents, this is far more difficult in the local constituency. Characteristically, fewer independents—and a smaller proportion of the independent vote—come from the local than from the national constituencies. In 1974, for example, while 13 percent of the national-constituency vote went to independents, in the local constituencies only 5 percent did so. Obviously the local constituencies are more difficult for independents to win and are therefore more politicized.

Moreover, the voter does not identify so easily with the larger constituencies of the House of Councillors as he does with the smaller constituencies of the lower house. This is reflected in the fact that the voting rate for the upper house is generally about 10 percentage points below that for the lower house. While the voting rate in the 1969 and 1972 lower house elections was 69 and 70 percent, the rate for the upper house election that came between the two in 1971 was only 59 percent. In 1974, the turnout for the Councillors election reached an all-time high of over 73 percent. Since the voter casts his ballot for the national and local constituencies at the same time, the voting rate is about the same. But there are always more invalid ballots for the national constituency, which suggests that the voters are less familiar with the national candidates than with the local, and care less about the national poll.

A further consequence of politicization has been the spread of lower house factionalism into the upper house. Basically, this results from the same conditions that have stimulated the "party-ization" of the upper house, namely the need for organized support in elections and in promotion up the political ladder. But the process was given an additional fillip by the 1956 LDP presidential election. When Kishi Nobusuke lost to Ishibashi Tanzan by seven votes, he decided to give more attention to building his support in the House of Councillors. An informal pro-Kishi group, the Seishin Club, was formed by Speaker Matsuno Tsuruhei, followed immediately by the formation of counter-groupings to represent the other factions in the LDP. Once these factional groupings came into existence, they controlled the appointment of upper house members to cabinet, party, and House posts.

15

But as some forces were whittling away the nonpartisan and independent character of the upper house, other forces continued to encourage some measure of distinctiveness. The fact that councillors are elected for a six-year term that is independent of the fate of the cabinet tends to make them less concerned than lower house members about routine party affairs. The lower house term is a maximum of four years, but in fact, as a result of Diet dissolution and election calls by the government, lower house terms have averaged only a little over two years since the end of World War II. A term of office that is about three times that of the lower house gives councillors, as their longer term gives U.S. senators, a very different political rhythm from that of the representatives. Because much can happen during their six-year term—including about three lower house elections—councillors are somewhat less pressed than representatives to make factional commitments, and more cautious about making them. In the case of an LDP member running in the local-constituency elections, for example, since the candidate must receive support from LDP members in all the lower house electoral districts of his prefecture—and these may be under the control of different factions—he must be careful not to antagonize any of them.

The record of upper house independence, which was one of the principal concerns of the system's framers, is not a happy one. During its heyday, the Ryokufūkai led a number of campaigns against government bills. One key point of leverage for the upper house is that it can delay a government bill (other than the budget or a treaty) for a considerable time. While it can be overruled by a two-thirds vote of the lower house, a two-thirds vote is no easy matter to achieve in view of the party distribution of seats in that house. The government party does not have the two-thirds by itself. Even if it did, it would still have to wait for the bill to go through the entire upper house procedure, which can take up to sixty days.

It is therefore often worthwhile for the government to compromise and accept some upper house amendments or, in very difficult cases, give in completely in order not to tie up other legislation. In 1952, for example, at the time of the explosively controversial Subversive Activities Bill, the Ryokufūkai's five amendments, passed by a majority of the House of Councillors, were accepted by the government and resulted in a very different application of the law from what might otherwise have come about. In 1954, the Yoshida cabinet was shaken by a Ryokufūkai resolution of admonition for its overruling the actions of the procurator's office. This came to be known as the "right of command case" (shikiken hatsudō). The constitutional question involved was whether public procurators were independent or under the command of the minister of justice; the government chose to interpret the law as allowing the minister to "supervise" the work of the public prosecutor. In April the minister had refused to approve the arrest of Satō Eisaku and Ikeda Hayato, two prominent conservative politicians (both later prime ministers), on suspicion of involvement in corrupt acts with shipbuilding companies. His refusal created a furor and, since the justice minister would not act on such an important matter without the approval of the prime minister, the Ryokufūkai's resolution of admonition was directed again the cabinet. The resolution passed with the support of opposition members and the justice minister resigned. The same year, Ryokufūkai amendments to two government education bills, supported by all the opposition parties from the Reform (Kaishintō) to the Communist, forced the government to compromise.

Since this high-water mark, however, the independence of the House of Councillors has ebbed. Today, there is virtually no difference in the political composition of the two houses. The small variations between the houses reflect only the differences in political mood at the time of their respective elections. For this reason the upper house elections are often regarded as indications of what is likely to come later in the politically more important lower house elections.

Nevertheless, some measure of upper house independence remains. The reelection of Kōno Kenzō to the speakership in 1974 is one sign of the continuing (if frail) spirit of independence of the upper house. Also, as shown in Table 1-1, the very fact that the two

Table 1-1

PERCENTAGE OF DIET SEATS HELD, BY PARTY, 1976

Party	House of Representatives[a]	House of Councillors[a]
LDP	56.0	51.2
JSP	23.2	24.8
KMT	6.1	9.4
JCP	7.9	7.9
DSP	4.1	3.9
Other	0.2	2.8
Vacant[b]	2.4	—

[a] As of February 1976.

[b] Through death, sickness, or resignation (twelve in the lower house, none in upper house).

Source: Summarized from *Kokkai binran*, 1976 edition.

houses are elected on a different time cycle means that they are very likely to differ slightly in composition. While the LDP currently holds 56 percent of the seats of the lower house, it holds only 51 percent of those in the upper house as a result of the 1974 election. To control all the upper house committees (that is, to hold all the chairmanships and a majority on each committee), the LDP would need 136 seats.[19] But the LDP holds only 129 seats. Since by upper house rule, the chairmen of standing committees cannot vote unless they step down from the chair,[20] the paper-thin LDP majority means there are several committees that it cannot control. Seven of the standing committees are now under opposition chairmen [21] (four JSP, two KMT, one JCP), the remaining nine under the LDP. The situation on committee control is as follows: the LDP is a minority on one committee (judicial affairs), that is, whenever the opposition unites, the LDP will be defeated; on four committees the LDP is a minority unless the LDP chairman votes, in which case it achieves parity; [22] in four of the committees chaired by the opposition, the LDP holds half the seats and therefore has a majority unless the opposition chairman votes, in which case there is an equal division.[23] On five committees the LDP has a majority, but only because the chairman will vote the LDP side to break a tie.[24] Only on social and labor affairs—chaired by the opposition—does the LDP wield an unconditional majority. But in these committees the majority is so small that difficulties are unavoidable. In December 1974, for example, the budget committee was deadlocked over the government's 1974 supplementary budget bill; the tie was broken by the chairman. In addition, since the speaker must be independent the number of LDP seats is further reduced by one. This situation will force the government to compromise or to drop programs that would be politically costly to get through the House.

The Broader Interest

Let us next look at how the concept of national as opposed to local representation has worked out over the Councillors' twenty-seven-

---

[19] See Watanabe Tsuneo, "Kyokoku renritsu seiken o mezashite," *Shinpū*, Spring 1975, p. 11.

[20] *Rules of the House of Councillors*, Article 45.

[21] JSP: social and labor affairs, communications, construction, audit; KMT: judicial affairs, transportation; JCP: discipline.

[22] Cabinet, local administration, foreign affairs, and agriculture-forestry-fishing.

[23] Transportation, communications, construction, audit, discipline.

[24] Finance, education, budget, house management, commerce and industry.

year history. It was noted earlier that under the Meiji constitution, the function of representing the national interest belonged to the House of Peers. Aside from the members of the peerage, who were automatically assumed to be acting in the interests of the nation as a whole, about one-fourth of the House of Peers consisted of Imperial appointees. It was among this group that the true transcendent national interest, the "sound element" of the country, the men of wisdom, learning, and experience, was found. In the final House of Peers, just before its dissolution and replacement by the new House of Councillors in 1947, 128 of the 373 members were Imperial appointees (as against 182 peers and 63 in the highest-taxpayer class). These were writers, scientists, scholars, top civil servants, and other commoners appointed for their achievements, their services to the country, and the honor they had brought to Japan. They included such people as Professor Minobe Tatsukichi of the Tokyo Imperial University Faculty of Law, the distinguished constitutional scholar who had been forced to resign in 1935 because his "organ theory" of the Emperor's position offended the militarists and extreme conservatives in the atmosphere that prevailed after the Manchurian Incident; Nanbara Shigeru, later the president of Tokyo Imperial University; and Abe Yoshishige, president of Gakushūin University.

Throughout the planning of the new upper house, many on the Japanese side were concerned with preserving at least this aspect of the House of Peers. But these distinguished figures were precisely those who would find the rough-and-tumble of ordinary electoral politics degrading. The national constituency, where they could run on their country-wide reputations, appeared to represent a possible solution.

The election of many such people in the first House of Councillors election seemed to confirm the expectations. But this first election was not the harbinger of things to come, but a fluke, perhaps an accident resulting from the tremendous confusion and fluidity of the early postwar days. As stability gradually returned to Japan, organizational rigidity began to set in. The process of politicization and the ever-mounting cost of elections quickly took their toll. By the second (1950) and particularly the third (1953) election these "national" personages had begun to drop away, either defeated in the elections or deterred from running by the cost and effort required. In place of the desired "national" figures, four new types of candidates have emerged: ex-bureaucrats; leading prefectural politicians; the so-called *tarento* ("talent") candidates (that is, entertainers, celebrities, and others prominent in the mass media); and representatives of national organizations and pressure groups.[25]

Ex-Bureaucrats. The participation of ex-bureaucrats in party politics is nothing new in modern Japan. In the early days of the prewar parliamentary system, the elected members of the Diet were regarded as representing the people and sectional interests while the bureaucracy was regarded as representing the nation as a whole. There was therefore a natural antagonism between the elected members and the bureaucrats. The bureaucrats conceived of themselves as serving not the government in power but the Emperor, the transcendent symbol of the nation. The higher civil servants in fact held their positions by imperial appointment and were awarded court ranks higher than those of Diet members. It is not surprising, therefore, that they counted heavily among the imperial appointees to the House of Peers. But once they overcame their distaste for party politics or, more accurately, once they came to realize that party politics had come to stay, many officials "went political." Ex-officials were prominent among the founders of political parties, Diet members, party functionaries, and cabinet ministers.

In postwar Japan high bureaucratic position has remained a significant channel into the Diet. Since 1946 between 25 and 35 percent of lower house members have been ex-officials. In the upper house as a whole the percentage is slightly lower, but for the LDP, much higher. About 40 percent of its local and over 50 percent of its national members are of bureaucratic origin. The national constituency is a particularly favorable arena for high-ranking ex-officials. For example, 41 percent of all the Ryokufūkai members in the first House of Councillors were ex-officials.

But ex-officials do not confine themselves to the national constituency; they stand in the local constituencies as well. An official may decide to stand in a local district rather than the national constituency for one of several reasons. He may believe that he can parlay his national reputation into "favorite son" status. He may have more political credit coming to him in the local constituency than he would nationally. Or he may judge that his official background has given him a solid local rather than a national base.

Higher civil servants, those at the bureau chief (*kyokuchō*) or administrative vice-minister (*jimu jikan*) level, are often in a position to establish politically useful personal connections throughout the

---

[25] This group, the representatives of national organizations, will be discussed in the sections following on proportional and functional representation.

country. In the first place, the ministries have national networks, so that a high-ranking official has a national organization of local branches of his ministry automatically available to him if he knows how to use it. In addition, because many ministries constantly perform favors for people all over the country (making purchases, issuing contracts, and so on) a skillful bureaucrat can build up a reputation through these contacts and lay up for himself credit that can later be drawn upon. Many corporations, pressure groups, business associations, and national organizations, as well as local entities, find it in their interest to have someone in the Diet who knows the bureaucratic ropes. They will therefore help with election funds and often with organizational support.

Hatoyama Iichirō—a successful candidate in the 1974 election—provides a good example of this process. Although Hatoyama has other obvious attractions, since he is the son of a former prime minister, his career has been spent in the public service. A graduate of the breeding ground of the higher civil service, the Faculty of Law of Tokyo University,[26] Hatoyama began his career in the Finance Ministry. After a break for military service during the war, he started up the bureaucratic ladder, through the posts of section chief and bureau chief, before ending up in the Economic Planning Agency as administrative vice-minister, the highest bureaucratic rank attainable. At fifty-five he retired from the civil service and ran in the national constituency. His candidacy in 1974 was supported by the Sumitomo group of companies, the Dai-ichi Kangyō Bank Group, several religious organizations, and many associations serving various industry interests or acting as lobbyists. With this support and his famous name, he won handily, coming in fourth highest in the national constituency.

The Construction Ministry, the Agriculture and Forestry Ministry, and the Japan Monopoly Corporation have the reputation of being election-wise. Finance Ministry officials, however, have their principal base among banking and financial interests, securities companies, and large corporations, and can count on substantial support from them. When the former administrative vice-minister of finance, Murakami Kōtarō, ran in the national constituency in 1971, his backers put on a spectacularly lavish campaign, one appropriate to a movie celebrity, replete with election campaign song—"Run, Kōtarō, Run!"—and brought him safely home eighteenth in a field of 106 candidates. In the 1974 elections, 8 of the LDP's 9 ex-bureaucrat national candidates won their seats, and 12 more won local seats.

---

[26] Until 1946, Tokyo Imperial University.

Bureaucrats constitute an important element in the Diet, though by no means the dominant one. Whether this meets the expectation that "men of knowledge and experience" would be drawn into the upper house remains a profoundly controversial issue. There can be no question that high officials have extensive understanding of national problems, of the work of government, and of the decision-making process. They have come from the top ranks of the best universities. In fact, the overwhelming majority have graduated from a single school, Tokyo University, and most of the rest from two or three others. They have survived a rigorous process of selection that has inevitably left them with the aura of an elite, but a deserving elite, who gain few material rewards. Not surprisingly, many think of themselves as dedicated servants of the nation.

At the same time, however, they are accused by their opponents of being narrow technocrats—aloof, arrogant, unable to grasp the needs and aspirations of the people, secretive, clannish, too close to the government in power, and incapable of independence or innovation. Many people profess themselves disturbed at the increased bureaucratization of the postwar legislature, which they see as a restoration of the prewar situation.

Still, the number of ex-officials in both houses of the Diet continues to rise, even if irregularly. Until 1957, about 40 percent of all cabinet members were ex-officials. Even the first (1972) cabinet of Tanaka Kakuei, whose great stock in trade was that he was not a bureaucrat, had one-third ex-official members.[27] By his third cabinet, formed in November 1974, one-half the members were of bureaucratic origin. The least bureaucratic of all postwar cabinets is the Miki cabinet of 1974 (six out of twenty ministers).

In the early 1960s there were proposals to prevent higher civil servants from using their official positions to political advantage by forbidding them to run in the national constituency in the first election after their retirement from office. But these proposals came to naught. Only three modest changes were made in the electoral laws affecting civil servants: the use of official position for electioneering purposes was forbidden, the use of official facilities or supplies for election purposes would be punished, and for an elected ex-official to give orders to former associates would invalidate his election.

The Locally Well-Known Men. If the national-constituency system was to favor the "well-qualified nationally famous leaders from all

---

[27] Three of the ten had had their bureaucratic experience before the war in the Manchukuo government or its agencies.

22

fields of endeavor,"[28] the new enlarged local constituencies, the framers hoped, would favor another desired category, the "locally well-known men."[29]

Although it has never been entirely clear who these people were to be, it is useful to try to identify them. In prewar Japan there was no single elective office from any constituency larger than the 120 or so small electoral districts into which the country was divided for the House of Representatives. Since each district elected several representatives, most seats were won with a small number of votes, averaging less than 15 percent of the vote in a district. It was hard to think of those elected by this process as truly national or even prefectural figures. There was no national election, like an American presidential election, because the prime minister was either appointed or elected indirectly by the members of the majority party in the Diet. Nor was anyone elected by the people at the next administrative level of government, the forty-seven prefectures, since prefectural governors were career civil servants appointed by the Home Ministry. The prefectural assembly was elected, but here again the electoral districts were small, so that no candidate was elected by a majority or a plurality of the people of the prefecture, as in U.S. gubernatorial elections. City, town, and village mayors were not elected by the people but indirectly by the local assemblies. Even the heads of Tokyo's wards were appointed by the governor of Tokyo.

After the war, the American Occupation's local-autonomy reforms made prefectural governorships, mayoralties, and ward headships elective. The new House of Councillors added two types of electoral district that were larger than what had existed in the past: the national constituency and the local constituency, which was prefecture-wide. For the first time it became possible for a public representative to be elected by a majority or a plurality of the voters in a geographic area larger than a small electoral district.

Election strategy in a large district differs greatly from that in a small district. For the lower house candidate running in a small multimember electoral district returning (say) five members, a special strategy is needed. Former Prime Minister Satō Eisaku, for example, won his 1972 Diet seat from Yamaguchi Prefecture's Second District with 66,000 votes, only 15 percent of the vote, and was second out of the five winning candidates. Since the prime minister is not elected by popular vote, as is the American president, this means that the prime minister who held office for the longest period in Japanese

---

[28] *Political Reorientation*, vol. 1, p. 183.
[29] Ibid.

history, eight years, was never judged by the people as a whole, but was elected by 15 percent of his own small constituency. Prime Minister Miki Takeo came in first in his five-member district in Tokushima Prefecture with less than 21 percent of the votes.

In 1972, the smallest winning vote total—Obuchi Keizō's 37,258 in Gumma's Third District—was just 9.59 percent of the votes. In low vote percentage, however, he was outdone by Ōno Ichirō in former Prime Minister Tanaka's Niigata Third District, who won with 9.09 percent (39,867 votes). The largest number of votes in the election (221,000) went to a Communist in Osaka's Third District, but even this was just 22 percent of the votes cast. The spread between the largest and the smallest number of winning votes for the House of Representatives in 1972 was therefore 1:5.93. Not a single representative won a majority of votes in his district, not even the winner in the only one-member district (Amami-Ōshima). The range ran from Ōno's 9.09 percent to Fukuda Takeo's 45.88 percent. Representatives won their seats with an average of about 60,000 to 70,000 votes.

This contrasts sharply with the situation of national-constituency candidates for the upper house. The lowest winning vote total in the 1974 election was 573,000—more than fifteen times the minimum required for victory in the lower house and over twice the maximum obtained there. The highest national winner was Miyata Teru, former television master of ceremonies, with 2.6 million votes. The record national-constituency total is held by writer Ishihara Shintarō, who won in 1968 with over 3 million votes. Yet, however impressive Miyata's victory, he was no truly nationally elected politician; his vote represented only 5 percent of the votes cast.

It is the local constituency of the upper house that provides the most favorable conditions for the locally well-known men. A comparison of the upper house local district and the lower house district suggests some of the issues involved. There are 123 lower house districts, of which 122 are multimember (between three and five members each) and one is single-member (Amami-Ōshima). For the upper house there are forty-seven districts (one for each prefecture), of which twenty-six elect one councillor, fifteen elect two councillors, four elect three, and two elect four.[30] Tokyo's voters elect thirty-nine representatives from ten lower house districts, but the same number of Tokyo voters choose only four councillors in a single upper house contest. Therefore, it was possible in 1972 for a representative to win

---

[30] Every three years one-half the members are elected for six-year terms. Each district therefore has twice the number elected at any one time.

a seat from Tokyo with as few as 46,000 votes (the highest vote being 208,000), but for the House of Councillors the lowest winning number was 820,000 and the highest 1,268,000. The minimum number of votes required in Tokyo to win an upper house seat was eighteen times larger than that required for winning a lower house seat. In spite of the far larger number of votes, the top winner in Tokyo in 1974, Yasui Ken, still only took about 23 percent of the vote. While he did not represent a majority of the Tokyo electorate, he still represented at least six times as many people as the highest winning representative. The smallest number of votes required to win an upper house local seat was in Yamanashi Prefecture, where Nakamura Tarō won with 177,000 votes. But whereas the highest winner in the lower house elections in Yamanashi took only 27 percent of the vote, Nakamura won his upper house seat with 42 percent, clearly a much higher degree of representation.

The closest to a true reflection of majority opinion is the single-member constituency. While in the lower house elections most representatives won with less than 20 percent and the highest percentage obtained was 46 percent (Fukuda Takeo, Gumma Third), in the upper house single-member districts, the winning vote ranged between 35 and 68 percent, with clear majorities in most districts.

Since prefecture-wide appeal is necessary to win in the upper house local elections, many prefectural governors or mayors of large cities, who have a proven appeal, stand as candidates. In gubernatorial elections there are usually only two major candidates, which means that one of them will win a majority, and often a huge majority. The governor of Tokyo, Minobe Ryōkichi,[31] who was supported by the JSP, the JCP, and the KMT, was elected in 1971 by the largest number of votes in Japan's history, 3.6 million, or 64.8 percent of the total. In only 4 of the 47 prefectures was the race won with less than a majority, and in largely rural Ishikawa Prefecture, Nakanishi Yōichi took 88.3 percent of the total. Just before the 1974 election, of the 152 locally elected councillors, there were 35 ex-officials, 29 labor union representatives, and 24 elected heads of local entities (governors and mayors). At least 39 of the local members also had experience in local assemblies. Those coming from a business background numbered 17. In 1974, the LDP ran 15 locally prominent candidates (8 governors, along with vice-governors and mayors) in the prefectural constituencies; 11 of them won, some by impressive margins. The JSP ran two ex-mayors, both of whom were also successful.

---

[31] The son of Professor Minobe Tatsukichi mentioned earlier.

One can conclude that the upper house constituency system makes it possible for some "locally prominent men" to win. But whether officials, governors, and mayors fit the "locally prominent" category better than teachers, journalists, professionals, cultural figures, and businessmen is perhaps a matter of taste. How they acquire a local base and why the parties like them, however, is clear.

Tarento. The planners' "locally prominent men" have turned out to be the local elected officials. The representatives of the "national interest" have increasingly been ex-bureaucrats. But what of the other distinguished national figures, the "best elements of the nation," the men of "learning and experience," who began to fade away from the scene so quickly after the first upper house election in 1947?

The most controversial of the new types that have arisen to replace them is the *tarento*, the media celebrities. They have been much deplored as a vulgarization of the high ideals of the planners. And polls confirm that the public looks upon them with jaundiced eye. In a survey taken shortly after the 1974 election,[32] 52 percent of a national sample of voters considered them "objectionable" as against 37 percent who considered them "unobjectionable." Except among young people (twenty to twenty-four years of age), disapproval was higher than approval in all groups in the population. This was as true of the supporters of the LDP, which relies heavily on the "talents," as of the opposition, which does use them, of course, but somewhat less than the LDP.

Nevertheless, the *tarento* have assets valuable in the diffuse national constituency that make it difficult for any party to forego their use, however distasteful this may be to their nobler political sentiments. The "talents" are well-known, popular, and attract the neutrals and the indifferent. The above poll showed that uncommitted voters, the voters who declare themselves independent or without party identification, object less to *tarento* candidates than does the general population.[33]

The *tarento*, in the sense of media celebrities, began to appear on the national political scene as early as 1953 when Ugaki Kazunari, a popular ex-army general, won first place in the national constitu-

---

[32] *Sangiin giin tsūjō senkyo no jittai seron chōsa kekka genshiryō—1974, 7-gatsu* (Tokyo: Kōmei Senkyo Renmei, 20 December 1974), pp. 269-286. National poll taken between 10-14 July 1974. Compare Curtis in this volume, p. 64.

[33] Ibid., p. 272.

ency. In 1959 the flamboyant Tsuji Masanobu ran third.[34] But the real breakthrough for the *tarento* candidates came in 1962 when a television star, Fujiwara Aki, won first place in the national constituency, the first time any candidate's vote total had topped the 1 million mark.

From then on the *tarento* candidate had to be reckoned with. In 1968 writer Ishihara Shintarō won first place with over 3 million votes, almost three times as many as the number two winner, Aoshima Yukio, a TV personality. (In 1974, Aoshima finished third with more votes, even though he very ostentatiously refused to campaign.) The four top 1968 winners were all *tarento*—two LDP, one independent, and one JSP (Ueda Tetsu).

Again in 1971, the three highest places were won by "talents," the first and third of whom ran under the JSP label. Of the top five winners in 1974, three fall into the *tarento* category and, if one includes Hatoyama Iichirō, who as the son of a former prime minister has a certain celebrity status, and independent Ichikawa Fusae, who could also be regarded as a celebrity, then the top six can all be so regarded (see Table 1-2). Of the thirteen *tarento* candidates, eight were elected. Four of the LDP's six *tarento* won.

The weight of the *tarento* votes in a party's overall total can be heavy: "talents" accounted for over one-fourth of all 1974 national-constituency votes cast for the LDP, for 10 percent of the JSP vote, and for almost half of the independent votes. In the 1971 election, the JSP's successful *tarento* contributed 55 percent of the party's national vote.

These huge votes are not necessarily a blessing. A large part must be regarded as overkill. The 2.6 million votes that elected one candidate, Miyata, in 1974, if distributed differently, could have won four more seats for the LDP. The Kōmeitō national candidates, by contrast, were tightly clustered between 625,000 and 800,000 votes (see Table 1-3). This tells us something about Kōmeitō efficiency. For the LDP the spread was between 574,000 and 2.6 million votes

---

[34] Tsuji, widely hailed as the "architect" of the Singapore strategy, had been a colonel in the Army's General Staff headquarters. At the end of the war, instead of surrendering himself to the Allied authorities, he went underground for five years, surfacing only in 1950. His best-selling *Senkō no 3000-ri* [Three thousand leagues in the underground] was an account of this period. Upon his return, he was immediately catapulted into national prominence, and he capitalized on this prominence to run for public office. After a stint in the lower house, he stood for election in the upper house national constituency in 1959. He left Japan on 21 April 1961 for parts unknown, but after July 1961, when he was reported to be in the Soviet Union, he disappeared from view, never to be heard from again. In 1962 another book of his, again a best-seller, was published.

Table 1-2

TOP TEN WINNERS, NATIONAL CONSTITUENCY,
HOUSE OF COUNCILLORS ELECTION, 1974

Candidate	Party	Background
1. Miyata Teru	LDP	TV master of ceremonies
2. Ichikawa Fusae	Ind.	celebrity, suffragette leader
3. Aoshima Yukio	Ind.	TV writer
4. Hatoyama Iichirō	LDP	ex-Finance Ministry; son of former Prime Minister Hatoyama Ichirō
5. Santō Akiko	LDP	actress
6. Saitō Eisaburō	LDP	commentator
7. Marumo Shigesada	LDP	hospital director
8. Kobayashi Kuniji	LDP	ex-Agriculture and Forestry Ministry bureau chief
9. Meguro Kesajirō	JSP	Locomotive Engineers Union
10. Tabuchi Tetsuya	DSP	Automobile Workers Union

Source: Based on Central Election Management Committee data.

Table 1-3

VOTES FOR KŌMEITŌ WINNERS, NATIONAL CONSTITUENCY,
HOUSE OF COUNCILLORS ELECTION, 1974

Name	Number of Votes	Rank
Miki Tadao	801,748	11
Suzuki Kazuhiro	758,910	14
Mineyama Akinori	756,183	15
Ninomiya Bunzō	714,968	19
Uchida Zenri	710,996	20
Fujiwara Fusao	676,226	27
Ōta Atsuo	675,336	28
Shiode Keisuke	640,623	39
Kambayashi Shigejirō	625,428	43

per winner.[35] Seven of the LDP candidates who just failed to make the winning fifty-four still had over 500,000 votes each. A little of Miyata's overkill vote might have brought several of them above the line.

How durable the "talents" will be it is still too early to say. The pattern so far is for a *tarento* to be elected once and then either leave politics or be defeated. Of the eight *tarento* winners in 1974, six were running for the first time and, if we exclude Ichikawa Fusae, who was perhaps a special case, only one *tarento*, Aoshima, has so far won a second term. The high winners of earlier years, Fujiwara Aki, Tsuji Masanobu, or Kon Tōkō, each lasted only one term. The most promising of the past *tarento*, the top 1968 winner Ishihara, decided to go more deeply into politics and won a seat in the lower house in 1972. In 1975, he ran for the governorship of Tokyo, but lost by a small margin.

Representation

Occupations and Interest Groups. A recurrent theme in the immediate postwar debate on the House of Councillors was functional, or occupational, representation. In the Japanese draft of February 1946,[36] the House of Councillors was to be "composed of members who are the representatives of various occupations. . . ." [37] This view, with minor variations, was shared by almost all the Japanese, the political parties as well as the various study groups. The Liberal party favored a system of occupational representation (along with Imperial appointment of men of "learning and experience"), as did the Socialist party (although without Imperial appointment).

The Japanese proposals, however, did not meet with Occupation approval. In the American view, occupational representation did not square with the principle of "direct election by the people." Further, as General Whitney put it, occupational representation smacked of Mussolini-style corporativism, and the Occupation was certainly not going to accept a fascist corporativist chamber. In the June 1946 Diet debates on the subject, State Minister Kanamori Tokujirō, then in charge of constitutional reform, was forced to acknowledge, in response to interpellations from the Representatives, that despite his desire for some form of vocational representation, there was not much chance it would come about.

---

[35] See Curtis in this volume, Table 2-3.
[36] Submitted to the Occupation in haste after the *Mainichi Shimbun* (1 February 1946) leaked what it claimed to be the position of the Matsumoto committee.
[37] *Political Reorientation*, vol. 2, pp. 605-606.

Nevertheless, even though a formal system of vocational representation could not be achieved, it was hoped that the proposed innovations, particularly the national-constituency system, would permit some vocational representation. Even the analysis of the Occupation's Government Section stated that the national-constituency system "favors election of locally well-known men and encourages selection of well-qualified nationally famous leaders from all fields of endeavor."[38] Although "all fields of endeavor" is not synonymous with "occupational representation," it is close. As far as the Americans were concerned, if some form of "occupational representation" did emerge under a system based on direct election, well and good.

The question then is whether it did emerge. Did the new House of Councillors make possible the representation of occupational interest groups? The results of the very first Councillors election of April 1947 show that 26 percent elected were representatives of organizations, and others such as religious workers and medical men were members of occupations they might be considered as representing. According to the American Occupation's analysis of the composition of the first House of Councillors, there were twenty-four farmers' association officials, twenty labor leaders, eight religious workers, five physicians, and ten women. In addition, twenty-two members were classified as teachers, a category including many who ran with the support of the teachers' union.

Not all of these members should, of course, be regarded as having been "representatives" of occupations or organizations, but many did fall in this category. Some of those listed as religious workers did, in fact, run as representatives of, and with the backing of, religious organizations desirous of some kind of representation. The Sōka Gakkai provides an example of religious representation: it started running candidates in 1956, first as independents and from 1962 under the label of Kōmei Seiji Renmei (Clean Politics League), the forerunner of the present Kōmeitō.

Diffuse national organizations or groups. Typically, these religious organizations, which include Buddhist leagues, Shintō associations, and several of the "new religions," such as Seichō, Tenrikyō, and Tenshō Daigu, as well as a variety of lay religious organizations (the Risshō Kōseikai, for example), are too weak in any single district to elect their own candidates, but they can aggregate their diffuse national support to elect a councillor in the national constituency. This is true of other kinds of organizations as well: national trade unions, medical associations, or the Sōka Gakkai.

[38] *Political Reorientation*, vol. 1, p. 183.

A good example is the *burakumin*,[39] or ex-touchables. They number somewhat over 1 million people—therefore between 700,000 and 800,000 voters—scattered throughout the country. Usually they comprise a few percent of the population in every electoral district. (Their highest concentration is in Hyogo Prefecture, where they may constitute as much as 10 percent of the electorate.) They are therefore unable to cluster enough votes to elect a member in any local constituency. But by concentrating their votes on one national candidate they can always win a seat, and by a respectable margin. In the first Councillors election of 1947, Socialist Matsumoto Jiichirō came in second in the national constituency and, because of his high vote, was chosen vice speaker of the House. In 1974, Matsumoto Eiichi, a Fukuoka businessman and *burakumin* leader, who had once served as the earlier Matsumoto's parliamentary secretary, was thirtieth among fifty-four national winners. Taking into account the national voting rate of about 73 percent, his 674,000 votes seem to be right on target, comfortably above the lower limit of 573,000 for election in the national constituency. In any local constituency, a *buraku* candidate would have had difficulty winning,[40] and even nationally more than one candidate would have divided the vote enough to defeat both of them. One candidate is exactly the right number to assure direct representation.

Other minorities or interest groups cannot muster enough votes from their own membership to elect a candidate. If they want to be represented, they must in effect buy a piece of a candidate who will be politically favorable to them. Every candidate tries to bring into his support structure such organizations and groups. Hatoyama Iichirō, mentioned above, provides a good illustration of how the process works. Hatoyama had the support of several organizations related to fields of activity in which he had been engaged as an official (for example, the Tobacco Growers Political League, the Sake Brewers Union, the Wholesale Sake Distributors Association, and the Forestry Association). All of these groups provided him not only with the

[39] Descendants of the untouchable groups of pre-Meiji Japan. In spite of their "emancipation" in 1871, they are still identifiable, living in segregated ghettos and discriminated against. Their numbers are estimated at between 1 and 2 million, living in almost 6,000 "communities," or *"buraku."* Hence the current euphemism *burakumin* or "buraku people." See George DeVos, *Japan's Invisible Race* (Berkeley: University of California Press, 1967).

[40] Aside from his home prefecture of Fukuoka, Matsumoto's vote was scattered throughout the country, from a low of less than 0.1 percent in Toyama to a high of 8 percent in Osaka. But even his high vote in Fukuoka, which netted him 28 percent of his total national vote, still represented only 9 percent of the total vote cast in Fukuoka. In the local elections there, 473,000 votes were needed to win; Matsumoto had 187,000.

votes of many of their own members but with a national support network that helped him campaign in a variety of ways. His financial support came primarily from Sumitomo companies, but also from the Dai-ichi Kangyō Bank Group. In addition, he was supported by one of the new, politically active, religious sects, the PL ("Perfect Liberty") Kyōdan. (See Appendix, Table A-7.) By backing Hatoyama (as well as several other candidates) the PL Kyōdan expected to have a friend in court.

Hosokawa Morihiro, one of the youngest councillors, who was elected in the national constituency in 1971 at the age of thirty-six, provides another example. Hosokawa is the scion of a famous aristocratic family of the pre-Meiji period: the Hosokawa lords of Kumamoto. After a brief career as a newspaperman, he launched his political career by running for the upper house. Apart from financial support, he secured the backing of a combination of small organizations each having diffuse support throughout the country: the Reiyūkai, a "new" religious sect; Ura Senke, one of the leading schools of the tea ceremony; the Japan Flower Arrangement Arts Association; and Japan's New Generation Society. None of these alone could have elected its own representative, but all could feel they had some representation through the aristocratic and youthful Hosokawa.

The parties' organizational support. The LDP and the opposition parties draw their organizational support from different sectors. The LDP occupational and interest group representatives usually come from (or are supported by) corporations, religious bodies, professional associations, and the more conservative civic organizations. Opposition candidates, insofar as they stand in a representative capacity, tend to come from trade unions, mass movements, and anti-establishment public civic associations.

In 1971, for example, of the twenty-one successful LDP national-constituency candidates, five could be regarded as directly representing interest groups—Japan Dental Association, Kajima Construction Company, Nursing Association, Veterans Pension Association, and Bereaved Families Association. But six other winners were supported by some religious organization, and almost all the rest were backed by some national organization. The representation of organizations is not, however, confined to the national constituency. Between ten and fifteen LDP councillors elected from the local constituencies may also be thought to represent occupational, professional, or interest groups. The 1974 picture is very much the same.[41]

---

[41] See Curtis, p. 65, and Blaker, pp. 98-105, in this volume.

If business, agricultural, religious, professional, and civic organizations bulk large on the LDP side, on the opposition side it is the trade unions that are strongly represented. The Sōhyō, Japan's largest labor federation, by and large supports the JSP. Its role is so great that many question whether the party controls Sōhyō or vice versa. In 1971, for example, of the eleven JSP national winners, four were trade unionists. In 1974, eight out of the ten JSP winners were trade unionists (the others being one *tarento* and one *burakumin* representative). The largest single group of labor union councillors are from the Japan Teachers Union, one of Japan's largest unions which has the kind of national network—reaching down into every city, town, and village—that is particularly useful in elections. Of the JSP's forty-six local councillors elected in the 1971 and 1974 elections, twenty-seven were trade unionists.

In the case of the DSP, the picture is even clearer: all of its national councillors are trade unionists, and all of them from the Dōmei, Japan's second largest labor federation. (There are only three local DSP councillors, none of them trade unionists.) On the other hand a different pattern exists among the JCP and Kōmeitō members. Among both, party officials constitute the largest number, although both also have a small number of *tarento*. On the JCP side, there are also representatives of national mass organizations.

Business and the elections. It is clear that business plays a key role in the elections, particularly on the conservative side. It is not so clear just what business buys with its money, though it certainly is not direct representation. Several well-known businessmen such as Kajima Morinosuke [42] and Fujii Heigo [43] have sat among the councillors. But they are not seated as "representatives" of big business. For them politics is a hobby or a form of public service. Big business (the *zaikai*) is generally quite opposed to the idea of candidates who stand as representatives of the business constituency.[44] In fact, most businessmen in elective office are relatively small entrepreneurs or officials of business organizations, such as chambers of commerce or trade associations. Top business leaders, typically relatively old and quite committed to their business interests, are unlikely to run.

---

[42] President of the Kajima Construction Company, founder of the Kajima Peace Awards. First elected in 1959, second in the national constituency; reelected with the highest vote in 1965. Did not run in 1971.

[43] Former vice-president of Yawata Steel Corporation, later president of Japan Steel Corporation; first elected from Gifu Prefecture in 1947, reelected continuously since then.

[44] In the lower house, Kosaka Tokusaburō, president of Shinetsu Chemical Company, is often regarded as a big business representative.

"Politics should be entrusted to politicians," in the words of Kikawada Kazutaka. "It is quite wrong for the party to depend upon corporations for both funds and candidates." [45]

It was this thinking that brought business leaders to reject an LDP proposal to run business candidates in the 1974 campaign. However, because, as one business leader warned, "we shall be in trouble if the LDP is unable to continue in power," [46] business support for the LDP campaign was expanded beyond the usual financial contributions to include organizational assistance as well. A number of companies in effect "adopted" national candidates and used their facilities to campaign for them. The *kigyō gurumi*—the "enterprise candidate"—became a major issue and, in the view of many, the public reaction against the practice had much to do with the LDP's election setback. [47]

Nearly every LDP national candidate had his corporation backing for financial and organizational support: Miyata, the Toyota Automobile Company; Hatoyama, the Sumitomo Group; Santō, the Hitachi Group; Saitō Eisaburō, the Fuyō Group, Kobe Steel, the Mitsukoshi Department Store, and the cosmetics industry; Kobayashi Kuniji, the land development industry; Satō Shinji, the Kajima Construction Company, Ube Industries, and Japan Cement; and so on.

Although the scale of this support was new, the practice was not. Large corporations had frequently backed individual candidates in past campaigns, particularly popular candidates who might bring some public relations benefits. The *tarento* candidates had been considered especially desirable. Shiseidō, Japan's leading cosmetics company, supported Fujiwara Aki, the top winner in 1962, and then Ishihara Shintarō, the top winner in 1968.

The unconcealed nature of business involvement in 1974 brought a barrage of criticism. A group of employees of New Japan Steel in Nagoya threatened to bring their company to court for having campaigned improperly on behalf of conservative candidates. But the heaviest criticism was directed against the Mitsubishi Group, which backed Saka Ken, an ex-police official. Saka's 516,000 votes were not quite enough to win him a seat, and he finished as the fifth runner-up. [48]

---

[45] President of Tokyo Electric Power Company and managing director of the Keizai Dōyūkai (Japan Committee for Economic Development), quoted in the *Asahi Evening News* (English language), 28 June 1974.

[46] Yasui Kizō, vice-president of the Keidanren (Federation of Economic Organizations), the single most important big business grouping in Japan, reported in *Asahi Evening News* (English language), 28 June 1974.

[47] See Curtis, p. 65.

[48] For details, see Curtis, pp. 66-69.

Criticism reached a high point shortly before the election. On 2 July 1974, just five days before the election, Horigome Masamichi, chairman of the Central Election Management Committee, issued a public blast denouncing the "enterprise candidate." Since Horigome was a leader of the JSP, the LDP accused him of improper partisan interference in the election and filed suit against him in the Tokyo District Court.

Also, as many observers pointed out, while Horigome took the enterprise candidate practice to task, he had not a word to say about the union candidates who are at least equally, and probably to a greater degree, controlled by their supporters. When a union decides to support a candidate, it contributes to his campaign from the union treasury and requires union members to vote for him. The Dōmei unions support the DSP and the Sōhyō unions the JSP. Ironically, it is the JCP that has been fighting for unionist "freedom of choice," while the JSP, which is the principal beneficiary of tight national union control, is battling to retain the present system. For Horigome to criticize the union-tied candidates would be tantamount to his deliberately goring his own ox. Nevertheless, the Horigome statement focused public attention on the issue of corporate involvement, and much to the disadvantage of the LDP, just before the election.

Women. Women may also be regarded as an interest group. Until the end of the war, Japanese women did not have the right to vote, much less run for public office. They were enfranchised in 1946, and one of the dramatic results of the first postwar elections was the appearance and the success of women candidates. Thirty-nine were elected to the House of Representatives in 1946, bringing women into the Diet for the first time in history. The number of women representatives declined in the following election (1947) and has remained steady between seven and twelve ever since. In the upper house, ten women were elected in 1947, eight from the national and two from the local constituencies. In 1974, eight were successful, giving a total of eighteen women councillors in all. Thus, still today in Japan, as in all other countries, few women run for election and still fewer win, in spite of the fact that women constitute a majority of the electorate.[49] And because women's participation in public affairs is still not fully accepted, those who run for office usually stand as women's candidates or representatives of civic organizations. If one thinks of "rep-

---

[49] Until 1968, the men's voting rate was always higher than women's. In that year's House of Councillors election, the women's rate overtook the men's and has remained higher ever since. Since there are more women than men, women are a substantial majority of the actual voters. (See Appendix, Figure A-2.)

resentativeness" as implying numbers proportionate to population, then women are underrepresented. But in terms of organized women, there is at least a modest degree of representation.

Proportional Representation. Occupational or interest group representation is only one aspect of proportional representation. In its broader sense Japan's electoral system has always aimed for proportionality. A single-member constituency system with the winners chosen by a straight majority (or plurality) would exclude many parties as well as other groupings from representation. As a general rule the larger the constituency base and the number of members to be elected, the greater the chance for true proportionality. The DSP, for example, won only 4.4 percent of the votes in the local constituencies in 1974. In a single-member, majority-winner system, it would have been eliminated. Its only 1974 local seat was won in a multimember district. In the national constituency, the DSP's 6 percent of the vote gave it 7.4 percent of the seats. Together with its seats left over from the 1971 election, the DSP has a total of ten upper house seats, 3.9 percent of the total, rather than none as might well be the case in a single-member district system.

The House of Representatives is elected from multimember districts (except for the island group of Amami-Ōshima). While the system allows minority parties to hold seats, representation is not fully proportional. The LDP, which won 47 percent of the votes in the 1972 House of Representatives election, occupies 56 percent of the seats, a commanding lead. The JSP is also slightly overrepresented, but the other three parties are all somewhat underrepresented (see Table 1-4).

The House of Councillors is elected differently. It has, it will be recalled, three different kinds of electoral districts: one-member local districts (twenty-six), multimember local districts (twenty-one), and the national constituency. The effect of district size on proportionality is quite clear, as illustrated in Table 1-5.

In 1974, the LDP won 49.6 percent of the votes in the twenty-six one-member districts. With this vote, it took twenty-four [50] of the twenty-six seats, that is, 92 percent. With 28 percent of the votes, the JSP took no seats at all.[51] In the two-member districts, the LDP won 47 percent of the seats with 43 percent of the votes. The JSP,

---

[50] In reality it took twenty-five since the "independent" winner in Tokushima later joined the party.

[51] In Okinawa, however, the winning candidate was a "progressive," supported by all the opposition parties.

Table 1-4

REPRESENTATIVENESS: HOUSE OF REPRESENTATIVES
ELECTION, 1972

Party	Percent of Vote[a]	Seats Won		Seats Currently Held[b]		Number of Seats Given Proportional Representation
		Number	Percent	Number	Percent	
LDP	46.8	271	55.1	275	56.0	230
JSP	21.9	118	24.0	114	23.2	107
JCP	10.5	38	7.7	39	7.9	52
KMT	8.5	29	5.9	30	6.1	42
DSP	7.0	19	3.8	20	4.1	34
Other	5.3	16	3.2	1	0.2	26
		491		479		491

[a] Elections, 10 December 1972.

[b] As of February 1976. By this time nearly all independents had joined parties and there were twelve vacancies, accounting for 2.4 percent of the seats.

however, did very much better: although it had exactly the same percentage of the vote as it had in the one-member districts—28 percent—it took 43 percent of the seats. The other parties were practically shut out, the KMT's 11 percent and the DSP's 2.5 percent gaining them nothing, and the JCP's 9 percent netting one seat, which is slightly over 3 percent of the thirty seats in the two-member districts. The three-member districts gave better proportional representation to the smaller parties. And in the four-member districts (Tokyo and Hokkaido), all the opposition parties but the DSP did better than the LDP with their smaller proportion of the vote. In the national constituency, which offers the best opportunity for proportional representation, there was a kind of reverse proportionality: the opposition parties all did better than their votes warranted, while the LDP took fewer seats than its vote warranted. Table 1-6 provides an overall picture of upper house "representativeness."

The problem of representation may also be viewed from the standpoint of the number of voters per seat. In a perfectly representative system, each seat would represent an equal number of voters. By this standard, Japan's upper house system is far from representative. For example, the number of voters per seat ranged from highs of 1,048,500 and 1,012,500 in the urban prefectures of Kanagawa

Table 1-5

PERCENTAGE OF VOTE AND SEATS WON, BY SIZE OF CONSTITUENCY AND PARTY, HOUSE OF COUNCILLORS ELECTION, 1974

Size of Constituency	Number of Constituencies	Party	Percent of Vote	Percent of Seats Won	Number of Seats Won
One-member	26	LDP	49.55	92.3	24
		JSP	28.15	0	0
		KMT	7.81	0	0
		JCP	10.65	0	0
		DSP	0.36	0	0
		Other	3.48	7.6	2
					26
Two-member	15	LDP	43.31	46.6	14
		JSP	28.24	43.3	13
		KMT	11.25	0	0
		JCP	9.00	3.3	1
		DSP	2.54	0	0
		Other	5.66	6.6	2
					30
Three-member	4	LDP	28.98	33.3	4
		JSP	20.13	16.6	2
		KMT	20.08	25.0	3
		JCP	17.17	16.6	2
		DSP	12.91	8.3	1
		Other	0.73	0	0
					12
Four-member	2	LDP	24.82	12.5	1
		JSP	23.99	37.5	3
		KMT	15.15	25.0	2
		JCP	15.39	25.0	2
		DSP	5.56	0	0
		Other	15.08	0	0
					8
National constituency	1	LDP	44.30	35.1	19
		JSP	15.18	18.5	10
		KMT	12.09	16.7	9
		JCP	9.37	14.8	8
		DSP	5.92	7.4	4
		Other	13.10	7.4	4
					54

Table 1-6

REPRESENTATIVENESS:
HOUSE OF COUNCILLORS ELECTION, 1974

Party	Percent of Vote	Seats Won		Number of Seats Given Proportional Representation
		Percent	Number	
LDP				
National constituency	44.3	35.2	19	24
Local constituencies	39.5	56.6	43	30
JSP				
National constituency	15.2	18.5	10	8
Local constituencies	26.0	23.7	18	20
KMT				
National constituency	12.1	16.7	9	7
Local constituencies	12.6	6.6	5	10
JCP				
National constituency	9.4	14.8	8	5
Local constituencies	12.0	6.6	5	9
DSP				
National constituency	5.9	7.4	4	3
Local constituencies	4.4	1.3	1	3
Other				
National constituency	13.1	7.4	4	7
Local constituencies	5.5	5.3	4	4

and Tokyo, respectively, to lows of 265,500 and 205,500 in rural Fukui and Tottori, respectively—with the national average being 496,000.

This disproportion is only slightly less in the House of Representatives—4.5 : 1 (Kagoshima's Second District versus Tokyo's Seventh) as against 5.1 : 1 in the Councillors. The imbalance is the subject of much debate in Japan. Since it clearly favors the LDP, which draws a disproportionate amount of its support from the rural areas and is relatively weak in the urban areas, the LDP strongly resists serious reapportionment. The LDP leadership, on the contrary, has for some time campaigned for a single-member constituency system, and in the 1974 Councillors election then Prime Minister Tanaka made this an important issue. At least at this stage, single-member districts would appear to favor the LDP (see Table 1-5).

If electoral districts are grouped by degree of urbanization, the overrepresentation of the rural areas is clear, as shown by Table 1-8.

Table 1-7

PERCENTAGE OF VOTE AND SEATS WON, BY TYPE OF CONSTITUENCY AND PARTY, HOUSE OF COUNCILLORS ELECTION, 1974

	Metropolitan		Urban		Semi-urban		Semi-rural		Rural	
	% of vote	% of seats won	% of vote	% of seats won	% of vote	% of seats won	% of vote	% of seats won	% of vote	% of seats won
LDP	34.3	35.7	41.9	31.2	50.9	83.3	52.5	73.3	51.2	63.1
JSP	12.0	14.2	16.7	43.7	14.0	8.3	17.2	26.6	17.4	21.0
KMT	14.5	21.4	12.5	12.5	11.5	0	10.6	0	9.4	0
JCP	13.8	28.5	9.5	6.2	7.6	0	5.5	0	7.0	0
DSP	6.2	0	5.8	6.2	6.4	0	5.6	0	5.6	0
Other	19.3	0	13.6	0	9.6	8.3	8.6	0	9.5	15.7
	100	100	100	100	100	100	100	100	100	100

Note: Compare classification and findings in Blaker, pp. 93, 105-107.

Source: My own calculations are based upon materials in Shakai Chōsa Kenkyūsho (Marketing Intelligence Corporation), and Nihon Seiji Sōgō Kenkyūsho (The Institute for Political Studies in Japan), eds., *Sangiin senkyo—shiryō to bunseki—1974* [Japanese upper house election—1974] (Tokyo: Shakai Chōsa Kenkyūsho, 1974), and particularly the chapter by Okino Yasuharu, "Senkyo kekka no ruikeibetsu bunseki," pp. 61-64. All prefectures were classified by the author according to degree of urbanization as follows:

Metropolitan: Tokyo, Kanagawa, Kyoto, Osaka, Hyogo.
Urban: Hokkaido, Saitama, Chiba, Aichi, Hiroshima, Fukuoka.
Semi-urban: Aomori, Miyagi, Ishikawa, Shizuoka, Nara, Wakayama, Yamaguchi, Ehime, Kochi, Nagasaki, Okinawa.
Semi-rural: Gumma, Niigata, Gifu, Mie, Okayama, Kagawa, Kumamoto, Oita, Miyazaki, Kagoshima.
Rural: Iwate, Akita, Yamagata, Fukushima, Ibaragi, Tochigi, Toyama, Fukui, Yamanashi, Nagano, Shiga, Tottori, Shimane, Saga, Tokushima.

The urban 54 percent of the population is represented by 39 percent of the seats; the nonurban 46 percent by 61 percent of the seats.

The result is a considerable disproportion in the number of voters represented by each seat of the different parties, as illustrated in Table 1-9. One locally elected LDP councillor represents 246,000 voters, while one DSP councillor represents 1,177,000, a difference of 4.8:1.

Whether one is to regard this disproportion as high or low depends on one's criteria. By American congressional standards the disproportion is high. By British standards [52]—in the British Parliament the disproportion in 1974 was more than ten to one—the Japanese system looks very fair. Compared to the U.S. Senate, where

Table 1-8

REPRESENTATIVENESS: DISTRICTS CLASSIFIED BY
DEGREE OF URBANIZATION, HOUSE OF
COUNCILLORS ELECTION, 1974

Type of District	Percent of Vote	Percent of Seats
Metropolitan	30.3	18.4
Urban	23.6	21.0
Semi-urban	14.6	15.7
Semi-rural	14.6	19.7
Rural	16.8	25.0

Table 1-9

REPRESENTATIVENESS: VOTES PER SEAT BY PARTY,
HOUSE OF COUNCILLORS ELECTION, 1974

Party	Average Number of Votes per Seat
LDP	245,532
JSP	385,891
KMT	672,776
JCP	647,519
DSP	1,176,698
Other	367,738

the disproportion between large and small states is on the order of sixty-two to one, the five-to-one disproportion of Japan's upper house looks reasonable.

Stability and Continuity

How would an observer looking out upon the present from the perspective of 1946–47 judge the outcome of twenty-seven years of operation of the House of Councillors election system? Clearly many developments, desirable or undesirable, that have taken place have resulted from the character of Japanese politics and the drift of public

[52] Richard Scammon, "The Election and the Future of British Electoral Reform," in Howard R. Penniman, ed., *Britain at the Polls: The Parliamentary Elections of 1974* (Washington, D.C.: American Enterprise Institute for Public Policy Research, 1975), p. 167.

opinion, rather than from the characteristics of the system itself. Let us look briefly at those developments that relate specifically to the postwar expectations about the upper house.

In April 1962, the two-party system appeared to be in the ascendant and upper house independence was at its lowest ebb, the Ryokufūkai had dissolved itself, and its successor, the Dōshikai, was reduced to a corporal's guard. At that time Satō Tatsuo, one of the original members of the Constitution Problems Study Committee, lamented: "The present House of Councillors is not what it was supposed to be. At this rate, we might as well have a unicameral legislature, or a system of recommended or appointed members. But the reasons for a two-house system are just as important today as they were then. . . ."[53]

But even if the House of Councillors' independence, as judged by the high standards of the framers, had declined, it was by no means entirely gone. Some differences exist between the two houses, even though not as great as those originally hoped for. The framers had hoped that the upper house would serve as a conservative restraint on the lower house, thereby helping to maintain stability and continuity. A purely popular representative body, they feared, could become radical, unstable, and irresponsible since it would be controlled by the political parties, who would be guided by partisan interest or by an all-too-fickle public opinion.

During its twenty-seven years the House of Councillors has not often acted independently of the lower house, given the similarity of party affiliation in the two houses since 1956 and strong party discipline. Nevertheless, there have been occasions where it has. What is ironic is that whenever the House of Councillors has acted independently, it has been against rather than for conservatism.

Does the House of Councillors provide the representation, geographical as well as functional, that its framers hoped it would provide? Geographically, there have been deviations from an ideal proportional representation system, though, on the whole, the deviations appear slight by comparison with those of other systems, and a moderate degree of proportionality is in fact attained. The principal imbalance results from the failure to reapportion electoral districts to adjust for population change. Since this issue is so tightly intertwined with the present balance of power among the parties, reapportionment is unlikely in the near future. The system does provide some functional representation for elements that would otherwise not be represented. The House of Councillors contains the national figures,

---

[53] *Asahi Shimbun*, 18 April 1962.

"locally prominent men," and representatives of specialized constituencies the planners envisioned. Doctors, dentists, nurses, veterans, war-bereaved families, and the *burakumin* are almost always represented. So are farmers, through the election of officials of agricultural organizations, and workers, through the election of labor union representatives. The educational world is represented by teachers union representatives on the left and officials of educational associations on the right. Business is represented by a few members, but more by the obligations incurred through its campaign contributions to candidates. Religious bodies are either represented directly, if they are strong enough (as in the case of Sōka Gakkai), or indirectly, through their support for particular candidates. Many civic organizations, from flower arrangement societies to lovers of opera and the martial sports, achieve some sense of representation by supporting candidates; as a result, they feel there is someone to whom they can turn or who understands their problems. Women find some representation through elected women members.

While one might debate whether the *tarento* are an adequate substitute for the distinguished intellectuals of the old House of Peers and even of the early House of Councillors, there are some councillors with whom the intellectuals can identify. Even the nonparty independent voters, including the so-called "post-political" (*datsu seiji*) group—those who have been turning away from politics—have their candidates. In 1974, Ichikawa Fusae, eighty-one years old, was one of them. So was the TV star Aoshima Yukio who went abroad during the elections and still came in third in the national constituency. In addition, some of the more intellectual of the *tarento* tend to attract independents who are disaffected with politics.

Very broadly, then, the system does seem to be doing what its supporters hoped it would do. The upper house is not simply a carbon copy of the lower house. Even if only slightly, the members of the Councillors are different from the Representatives.

2

THE 1974 ELECTION CAMPAIGN: THE POLITICAL PROCESS

Gerald L. Curtis

The analysis of campaign practices and candidate strategies has a particular importance in the study of present day Japanese politics. Through most of the postwar period Japanese political forces were severely polarized, with a "conservative camp" on one side and a "progressive camp" on the other side of a sharply defined ideological cleavage. The political opposition was led by the Japan Socialist party and the whole system was dominated by the conservative Liberal Democratic party. Today ideological polarization is breaking down and the party system is becoming more complex. During the past decade the LDP has continued to control a majority of seats in both houses of the Diet but its popular support has steadily declined. At the same time, the JSP has suffered setbacks at the polls and the Kōmeitō and the Japan Communist party have established themselves as important parties of opposition. The result is a party system in greater flux than at any point since the mergers of the conservative and socialist parties into the LDP and JSP twenty years ago.

In this fluid and more highly competitive system, campaign strategies and tactics take on a new importance. There are many Japanese voters who identify strongly with one or another of the five political parties (the fifth being the Democratic Socialist party). But there is also a large and growing number of "floating" voters whose performance at the polls, if they vote at all, can be significantly affected by the skill with which parties and candidates make their appeal.

The author wishes to express his appreciation to the news staffs of the Fuji Telecasting Company and Fuji affiliates in Nagoya and Osaka for the generous assistance they gave him during his study of the campaign.

45

Party Policies and Postures

The LDP entered the 1974 upper house campaign on the defensive. Its popularity had declined steadily in previous elections and it was being attacked because of high prices, pollution, inadequate social services, and a variety of other issues of public concern. Prime Minister Tanaka's popularity had sunk to a point lower than that of any other postwar prime minister. According to one survey, only 22 percent of the electorate supported his administration on the eve of the election.[1]

For most of its history the LDP had not faced a serious challenge in national Diet elections. Even now it controls some 56 percent of the seats in the lower house and it went into the 1974 election with a small majority of seats in the upper house as well. But support for the party has steadily eroded. In the 1967 lower house election the LDP failed for the first time to receive a majority of votes and its popular support declined further in the two subsequent general elections. The party's vote has also fallen steadily in the upper house local-constituency and in gubernatorial, mayoral, and local assembly elections. But the 1974 upper house election marked the first time in LDP history that the party had entered a Diet campaign not entirely certain that it would be able to return enough candidates to maintain a majority of seats.

As suggested by its official campaign slogan, "To Protect Free Society" (jiyū shakai o mamoru), the LDP tried to portray itself as the one party fully committed to the parliamentary process, civil liberties, and a free enterprise system. Party leaders stressed the dangers of increased Communist influence if the LDP were to lose its majority and, in some of the more heated moments of the campaign, appeared to be equating the survival of freedom itself with LDP success. The efforts of at least a few LDP leaders were directed at trying to reconstruct a sharp and simple ideological cleavage in the society, to portray the issues at stake in the election as extreme and fundamental and thereby draw erstwhile LDP voters back into the conservative camp and the party's supporters to the polls.

The party leadership also attempted to rally support against the opposition on several specific issues. Prime Minister Tanaka pushed a "law and order" issue, demanding more stringent enforcement of the laws prohibiting workers in public enterprises and teachers from striking. Just before the campaign got underway, several Japan Teachers Union leaders were arrested for leading an illegal strike.

---

[1] *Yomiuri Shimbun*, 1 July 1974 (see Blaker, pp. 84-85).

During the campaign, Tanaka proposed legislation requiring all teachers to take a loyalty oath. He also reiterated his proposal for changing the electoral system for the lower house to a single-member-constituency system. This reform ostensibly would result in less expensive campaigns but, from the perspective of the opposition, it seemed to be an attempt to eliminate some of the opposition parties and increase the LDP majority. While trying to rally support against the opposition on these issues, the LDP also moved to adopt as its own several of the opposition's most popular issues, particularly those relating to social services and government social welfare expenditures. But, in part at least, the thrust of the Tanaka-led LDP campaign effort was to raise the spectre of radical change in the event of an LDP loss of its majority position in the upper house and to draw conservatively inclined voters back to the LDP and to the polls in large numbers.

When the election campaign began, voter interest was centered on the issue of inflation. Some 61 percent of those sampled in one poll [2] were primarily concerned with high prices, an increase from 41 percent in a similar poll taken before the 1971 election. No other issue stood out so prominently in preelection surveys. Although foreign policy issues related directly to Japan's inflation problem, they received scant attention from the electorate and from the candidates. The security treaty with the United States was largely ignored in the campaign and military and defense issues were hardly debated. In the poll cited above, only 0.4 percent of those polled expressed concern with defense issues, a decline from 7.8 percent in 1971. Twelve percent of this sample indicated primary interest in issues of social welfare, up four percentage points from 1971. The pollution issue, which before the 1973 oil boycott had drawn major public attention, was far overshadowed by the dominant concern with inflation. Only 4.8 percent of those polled mentioned pollution, compared to 15 percent at the time of the election three years earlier.

Although public concern with inflation was intense, the opposition parties were limited in their ability to attack the LDP effectively on this issue. Many people seemed to agree with the ruling party that enormous price rises were the consequence of developments beyond the control of the government—namely the Arab oil boycott and the extraordinary increase in oil prices. The opposition criticized the government but did not offer specific solutions that sounded more realistic or more palatable than the policies the government was adopting. Without remedies of their own to suggest, the opposition

[2] Ibid. (compare with Blaker, pp. 82-83).

party candidates kept their attacks on LDP economic policies on a rather general level. The campaigns of the opposition parties, much like that of the LDP, concentrated less on putting forth specific proposals on policy issues than on trying to convey a particular "posture."

The Opposition Parties. Although LDP popular support has declined steadily over the past decade, support for the largest opposition party, the Japan Socialist party, also has slipped. Many observers expected that the JSP would lose ground in the 1974 upper house election and that if gains were to be made against the LDP they would be made by the Kōmeitō and the Japan Communist party. For the JSP, the 1974 election was particularly crucial. For the first time there was a chance of the LDP's losing its majority in the upper house. This possibility of a "reversal of the conservatives and the progressives" (hokaku gyakuten) itself became an important campaign issue. The JSP stressed that hokaku gyakuten was the first crucial step toward creating a united opposition coalition government centered around the JSP and based "on the principles of protection of the constitution, democracy, neutrality and the improvement of life."[3] Its official platform addressed a number of issues, calling for higher social welfare expenditures, an end to inflation, a five-day work week, stricter anti-monopoly laws and a "democratization" of industry, rejection of Tanaka's regional development plans, and a strong public housing policy. But rather than fully developing any of these issues, JSP candidates—at least those whom the author had the opportunity to listen to—tended to place greatest emphasis on trying to convince the voters that only the JSP could serve as a "linchpin" to connect and hold together all the progressive and democratic forces in Japanese society.

The relative lack of attention to specific alternatives to LDP policy also characterized the campaigns of the other opposition parties. The Kōmeitō platform suggested that inflation could be controlled by ending a high-growth economic policy that favored big business; it called for increased government support for small- and medium-sized industry, higher social welfare expenditures, greater agricultural self-sufficiency, opposition to the adoption of a single-member-constituency system in the lower house, and, in foreign policy, "peace, autonomy, and neutrality." But KMT candidates spent little time developing the party's policy line and much time trying to convince the voters that, as the party of "freedom and humanism,"

---

[3] This discussion of party policies is based on the official party platforms published in the Asahi Shimbun, 14 June 1974.

the Kōmeitō was the only clearly anti-Communist and at the same time progressive and dynamic party running in the election.

The Democratic Socialist party devoted most of its efforts to fostering an image of realistic and pragmatic liberalism. Under the banner of "constructive progressivism" DSP candidates stressed the party's integrity and independence and its refusal to engage in electoral cooperation with the JSP and the KMT, at least until the JSP rejected all forms of alliance with the JCP. The domestic policy platforms of the opposition parties were broadly similar but the DSP placed greater emphasis than the other parties on educational reform, criticizing the LDP for having failed to bring about needed reforms and the JSP for having used the Japan Teachers Union to inject politics into the educational process. In foreign policy the DSP continued to support a policy closer to that of the LDP than to the policies of the other opposition parties. It called for the continued development of a modest Japanese military capability and the retention of the security treaty with the United States, but with the phasing-out of American military installations in Japan.

The Japan Communist party came into the election on the upswing. Its popular vote in the past several elections and its number of seats in the lower house had risen dramatically, and it had become a significant political force. Thanks in part to the LDP portrayal of the election as a confrontation between the LDP and the JCP, the Communists, with only ten upper house seats, entered the campaign with the image of a serious challenger. The JCP's lack of parliamentary strength could be turned to advantage by arguing that, unlike the JSP, it was not the "establishment's opposition" and, unlike the KMT and the DSP, it was not a conservative party in disguise. The Communists tried to convey the image of a party committed to the democratic process and concerned with Japanese national interests. The JCP's moderate, peaceful, and nationalistic line was summed up by the slogan "three freedoms." Each "freedom" was the JCP's answer to one of the three major attacks on the party: that it sought radical transformation of the Japanese economic system; that it would eliminate civil liberties and the parliamentary system; and that it would ally Japan with Communist states in its foreign policy.

The first "freedom" was the right to a decent standard of living. Within this category were included the domestic policy positions the party supported: social welfare, stronger government controls on business, and other policies almost identical to those advocated by the other opposition parties. The JCP, however, paid greater attention to the problem of the farmer than it had in previous elections.

Realizing that its rate of growth in popular support in the cities was likely to slow down, the party appeared to be making a new effort toward building support among the farming population. JCP candidates in rural areas took a stridently protectionist line, sounding remarkably like LDP candidates a decade earlier, before the LDP government adopted a wide variety of trade liberalization measures including the liberalization of some agricultural imports.

The second JCP freedom concerned civil liberties—freedom of speech, thought, and the press. This second freedom placed the party officially in opposition to political violence and revolution and in favor of a parliamentary form of government. The party stressed its independence from other Communist parties and its willingness to work peacefully within the "rules of the game" of parliamentary democracy.

The third freedom was "national freedom" (*minzoku no jiyū*), a phrase reflecting the strong nationalistic theme of the party's platform. The party urged cooperation with "the peace loving forces in the world," abolition of the security treaty with the United States, and neutrality. Unlike the Socialists, the JCP did not advocate unarmed neutrality for Japan but a defense policy that at least implicitly would permit Japan to maintain a sizable military force.

All the opposition parties devoted their energies in the campaign to convincing the voters to effect a "reversal of the conservatives and the progressives." But they were not yet prepared to tell the electorate what specific goals they would hope to accomplish and what specific policies they would adopt were they to find themselves in control of the government. In their platforms and campaign speeches, they remained parties of protest.

Rhetoric and Reality in Opposition Party Cooperation. Various attempts have been made in recent Japanese elections to achieve some degree of cooperation among the opposition parties. The JSP and the JCP have jointly sponsored a number of candidates in gubernatorial and mayoral elections and have scored impressive victories in a number of major urban areas. They have not, however, cooperated in the support of candidates in national elections. In the 1974 upper house campaign the JSP organization in Kochi Prefecture officially supported the local JCP candidate but this was done without any anticipation of electoral success and was a minor exception to a pattern of JSP-JCP competition in national elections. In districts where joint sponsorship of candidates might have resulted in the defeat of LDP candidates, JSP-JCP cooperation failed to materialize.

The JSP, KMT, and DSP have combined their support for candidates in a number of elections. The 1971 upper house election marked the high point in cooperation among these three parties in national elections when they officially pooled their efforts behind JSP candidates in three districts (Oita, Shimane, and Tochigi) and unofficially behind another (in Gifu). The JSP won in these four districts as well as in four other rural constituencies where the KMT and the DSP did not run candidates. Through these means, the opposition was able to make the deepest inroads ever into the heart of LDP support. In 1971, the LDP won only sixty-two seats, eight fewer than the seventy promised by the then secretary-general and later prime minister Tanaka Kakuei.

The success of electoral cooperation in 1971 generated considerable speculation about the possible emergence of a new opposition party that would encompass elements of the JSP, the KMT, and the DSP. In the following years, however, the prospects for such party reorganization steadily faded. In the 1974 election the DSP rejected all forms of opposition-party cooperation and the joint efforts by the JSP and the KMT in four districts were marked by a notable lack of enthusiasm in party headquarters and friction at the local level. What happened after the 1971 upper house election to turn the tide away from cooperation among these parties?

When the JSP, KMT, and DSP cooperated in the 1971 upper house election, the JSP appeared to be moving toward a split between its moderate faction led by Eda Saburō and the left wing of the party. Sōhyō, the labor federation supporting the JSP, and Dōmei, the labor organization backing the DSP, were discussing the creation of a liaison council and the possibility of future amalgamation. The KMT was still reeling from a scandal arising from its attempt to prevent the publication and then sale of a book critical of the party. It was also weakened by the formal separation of the party from its parent organization, Sōka Gakkai. The DSP, struggling to stay alive after the sudden death of its chairman, was showing serious interest in forming a new party that would include elements of the JSP. There were incentives for all of these parties to try selected cooperative campaigns in the 1971 election as a step toward the possible reorganization of the parties of the non-Marxist left. As stated earlier, the result was the victory of all the JSP candidates supported by the KMT and the DSP. The JSP, which had obtained only twenty-eight seats in the previous upper house election, won thirty-nine in 1971.

Soon after the 1971 election, relations among these three parties began to deteriorate. The right-wing elements of the JSP could neither muster the courage to break away from the party nor convince the party leadership to forsake political alliances with the JCP in favor of closer cooperation with the KMT and DSP. The JSP's verbal battles with the KMT and DSP on the one hand and with the JCP on the other became increasingly bitter. The disarray within the "progressive camp" worsened in the spring of 1974 during the Kyoto gubernatorial campaign. The local JSP organization was split on support for the incumbent governor, who had previously been elected as the joint JSP-JCP candidate but who seemed to his critics more Communist than Socialist. Another JSP candidate entered the fray to find himself the recipient of the support not only of much of the local JSP organization, but also of the KMT, the DSP, and the LDP as well, since the LDP had no hope of running a winning candidate and saw an opportunity to defeat the long-powerful incumbent. The internal JSP fight became so bitter that the national JSP organization intervened, ordering that the party's endorsement be given to the incumbent JSP-JCP candidate. The other candidate then decided to run as an independent, touching off conflicts within the local JSP organization, between the local and national JSP organizations, and among all the opposition parties. The incumbent won by a narrow margin but the controversy left its scars on the JSP and reinforced throughout the nation the image of a disordered and incoherent opposition. In short, by the time of the 1974 upper house election, the much professed goal of "opposition party cooperation" (yatō kyōryoku) had lost its credibility.

Furthermore, each opposition party had compelling reasons to minimize joint party cooperation in the 1974 election—reasons which it had not had in 1971. The KMT, having weathered the most difficult period in its short history (caused by the book scandal and the break with Sōka Gakkai), believed that it had stabilized its support and should turn to building and expanding the party organization. Its expectation of winning seats was modest, but party leaders saw the race as an opportunity to strengthen the party's national organization, to expand the party into new districts where it had not previously been active, and to build local support in anticipation of the lower house elections expected in 1976. Thus, while party spokesmen talked of the desirability of opposition party cooperation, the party selected thirty-six candidates to run in the local constituencies, including seventeen one-member districts where there was no chance of victory and where the only conceivable short-term effect would be the defeat of JSP candidates. Part of the party's strategy in running so many candidates apparently was to convince the JSP to abandon joint efforts with the JCP in favor of cooperation with the KMT. By supporting three JSP candidates (the JSP supported one KMT candidate), it kept the door open to more ambitious cooperative campaigns in the future; by running thirty-six of its own candidates, it built its local organization for the next lower house election and signaled the JSP that it had the votes that could spell the difference between victory and defeat for Socialist candidates in many districts.

For the DSP the issue of cooperation with other opposition parties posed problems different from those it posed for the KMT. DSP popularity is so low and localized that the party cannot effectively play a spoiler's role, as can the KMT. It cannot withdraw its own candidate in favor of helping a JSP candidate in districts where DSP support is high enough to make such an offer meaningful, because it needs to elect every member it can to maintain the minimal number of seats necessary to stay alive politically. A party with less than ten members in the upper house is not recognized as a party and loses all rights to participate as a "parliamentary negotiating group" (*innai kōshō dantai*). Rather than joint cooperation, the DSP's objective now appears to be to maintain its present Diet strength, to plant itself squarely in the political center, and to play a crucial role in a coalition government when the LDP's Diet majority disappears and a coalition becomes unavoidable.

The Communist party's public position on joint opposition-party activities has been to support a united front of all "progressive forces." Nevertheless, although it has stressed electoral cooperation with the JSP in its rhetoric, the JCP ran candidates in a number of districts in the 1974 election where the only possible consequence would be the defeat of Socialist candidates. The JCP, like the KMT, used the upper house election as an opportunity to build its local organization and support for the next lower house election. To many of its critics, JCP strategy seemed designed primarily to weaken the JSP, thereby strengthening the JCP's position relative to that of the other opposition parties. With popular support for the Communists growing, the JCP was less interested in fostering cooperation with the other opposition parties than in increasing its own representation in the Diet.

Choosing the Candidates

One obvious crucial decision Japanese political party leaders must make in an election is the number of candidates to run. The factors influencing such a decision are complex. Some parties run only candidates who stand some chance of winning; others run candidates even where defeat is certain in order to build support for later elections and to keep the political machine oiled. The number of candidates a party runs is affected by such factors as pressures from within the party and its supporting organizations and the amount of campaign funds available. While the cluster of factors involved in a particular case will vary, all strategic decisions concerning the number of candidates are made within the context of a specific electoral system. Each of the electoral systems in Japan—the one for electing members to the lower house and the local and national-constituency systems for the upper house—requires markedly different endorsement strategies.

Strategies in the National Constituency. Each party uses different strategies to win in these several constituency systems. In the upper house national constituency,[4] the JCP and the Kōmeitō, for example, employ a similar strategy for determining how many candidates to endorse. That strategy is to estimate the total national vote for the party and run only as many candidates as are expected to win. While this approach may seem like common sense, it is quite different, as we shall see, from the approach employed by the LDP. As Table 2-1 shows, the JCP and KMT have maintained a 100 percent success rate in the national constituency in the past five upper house elections, including 1974.[5] The KMT's representation in the upper house through the national-constituency elections has remained virtually unchanged for the past decade. It ran seven candidates successfully in 1962 and nine in the 1965 and 1968 elections. In 1971, after officially severing its relationship with the Sōka Gakkai, the party again ran nine candidates. JCP practice has likewise been to avoid running more candidates than are likely to be elected. But the Communists have steadily increased their number of Diet members elected through the national constituency. Beginning with two winners in the 1965 national-constituency election, the JCP won three seats in 1968, five seats in 1971, and eight seats in 1974. During this 1965–1974 period, its share of the vote in the national constituency rose from 4.4 to 9.4 percent.

Both the JCP and the KMT employ what Japanese refer to as a "horizontal" (*yokowari*) strategy for the national constituency. The country is divided into regions and each candidate's publicity and campaign activities are restricted to the prefectures in his assigned

[4] For a description of the national-constituency system, see Passin, pp. 1, 8, and 29–34 in this volume.

[5] Figures are given only for the five elections since 1962 because the KMT (then the Kōmei Seiji Renmei) and the DSP ran for the first time in the 1962 upper house contest.

Table 2-1

CANDIDATES ENDORSED AND ELECTED, BY PARTY, HOUSE OF COUNCILLORS ELECTIONS, 1962–1974

	LDP	JSP	KMT	DSP	JCP
1962					
National constituency					
Number endorsed	39	19	7	5	2
Number elected	21	15	7	3	2
Percent elected	53.8	78.9	100.0	60.0	100.0
Local constituencies					
Number endorsed	61	50	2	19	45
Number elected	48	22	2	1	1
Percent elected	78.7	44.0	100.0	5.3	2.2
All constituencies					
Number endorsed	100	69	9	24	47
Number elected	69	37	9	4	3
Percent elected	69.0	53.6	100.0	16.7	6.4
1965					
National constituency					
Number endorsed	36	16	9	5	2
Number elected	25	12	9	2	2
Percent elected	69.4	75.0	100.0	40.0	100.0
Local constituencies					
Number endorsed	59	50	5	16	46
Number elected	46	24	2	1	1
Percent elected	78.0	48.0	40.0	6.3	2.1
All constituencies					
Number endorsed	95	66	14	21	48
Number elected	71	36	11	3	3
Percent elected	74.7	54.5	78.6	14.2	6.2
1968					
National constituency					
Number endorsed	34	15	9	4	3
Number elected	21	12	9	4	3
Percent elected	61.8	80.0	100.0	100.0	100.0
Local constituencies					
Number endorsed	59	47	5	12	46
Number elected	48	16	4	3	1
Percent elected	81.4	34.0	80.0	25.0	2.2

Table 2-1 (continued)

	LDP	JSP	KMT	DSP	JCP
All constituencies					
Number endorsed	93	62	14	16	49
Number elected	69	28	13	7	4
Percent elected	74.2	45.2	92.9	43.6	8.2
1971					
National constituency					
Number endorsed	34	13	8	4	5
Number elected	21	11	8	4	5
Percent elected	61.8	84.6	100.0	100.0	100.0
Local constituencies					
Number endorsed	59	47	2	7	46
Number elected	41	28	2	2	1
Percent elected	63.5	59.6	100.0	26.6	2.2
All constituencies					
Number endorsed	93	60	10	11	51
Number elected	62	39	10	6	6
Percent elected	66.7	65.0	100.0	54.5	11.8
1974					
National constituency					
Number endorsed	35	12	9	5	8
Number elected	19	10	9	4	8
Percent elected	54.2	83.3	100.0	80.0	100.0
Local constituencies					
Number endorsed	60	45	36	9	45
Number elected	43	18	5	1	5
Percent elected	71.7	40.0	13.9	11.0	11.0
All constituencies					
Number endorsed	95	57	45	14	53
Number elected	62	28	14	5	13
Percent elected	65.3	49.1	31.1	35.7	24.5

Source: Adapted from Fuji Telecasting Company, *Documents for the 10th Upper House Election*, 7 July 1974. For further data, see Appendix, Table A-4.

region. Stringent measures are taken to insure that a candidate's campaign does not "spill over" into an unassigned area. The JCP newspaper, *Akahata*, for example, puts out special one-sheet editions during the campaign and voters in any one prefecture will receive only copies of the paper carrying the picture and story of the candidate assigned to that prefecture. This horizontal strategy is particularly suited to parties with strong local party organizations.

The JSP, which must rely on the nationwide memberships of supporting organizations for votes in the national constituency, combines a horizontal with a "vertical" (*tatewari*) strategy, the latter based on the support of members of Sōhyō-affiliated labor unions. The high-water mark for the JSP in the national constituency was in 1962 when it ran fifteen of its nineteen candidates successfully. A declining vote since then has forced the party to reduce the number of its national-constituency candidates. In the 1974 election the Socialists ran only twelve candidates.[6] One of the twelve was a "talent" or celebrity candidate, a well-known former television newscaster, Hata Yutaka, who was running for the first time. Hata concentrated his campaign in metropolitan areas and, in addition, received the support of three Sōhyō unions. Another JSP candidate, Matsumoto Eiichi, ran with the backing of the Buraku Kaihō Dōmei, the organization of Japan's outcast *burakumin* group, and focused his campaign in Kyushu and that part of the Kansai region where many *burakumin* live. He also was given the support of the private railway workers unions in these areas. All other JSP candidates ran as representatives of particular Sōhyō-affiliated labor unions.

The DSP national-constituency campaign was small—five candidates, all but one of whom ran as representatives of particular Dōmei-affiliated labor unions. With so few candidates, and no candidates sharing the support of the same union, there was no point in assigning particular regions to the candidates. Each endeavored to mobilize the support of the membership of the union backing him. The unions promoting successful DSP candidates were those in the textile industry (Karatani Michikazu), automobile industry (Tabuchi Tetsuya), electric equipment and chemical industry (Mukai Nagatoshi), and the Maritime Workers Union (Wada Haruo).

The cautious endorsement strategies followed by all the opposition parties in the national constituency simplified the LDP's endorsement policy considerably. Even if all opposition candidates had been elected in 1974, there still would have been twenty seats left unaccounted for. Although many non-party-affiliated candidates ran, only five or six were serious candidates, the rest being what Japanese call "bubble candidates" (*hōmatsu kōho*), who pop up and pop out without any chance of being elected. Thus, any LDP politician looking

---

[6] These candidates with their organizational backing and the geographical areas in which their campaigns were to be concentrated are listed in Table A-9 of the Appendix.

at the opposition candidates could guess with fair accuracy what the range of LDP possibilities would be. In 1974 the range was widely perceived as between eighteen and twenty-two seats. With eighteen "safe" seats, the LDP leadership was buffeted by conflicting pressures as to how many candidates to run. On the one hand, incumbents want as few candidates as possible because of their fears, well justified by experience, that fielding many new candidates could defeat them, despite a victory for the party as a whole. On the other hand, faction leaders demand the endorsement of new candidates, and a variety of organizations which support the LDP urge endorsement of "their" candidates.

Virtually without exception, it is LDP policy to endorse all incumbents who want to run. Although aged LDP incumbents were informally pressured to step aside, fourteen incumbents and two former upper house members were endorsed by the party in 1974. The total number of LDP candidates, however, was thirty-five, roughly the same number the party has run in the past several elections. In the 1974 election nineteen of these LDP national-constituency candidates were successful. But eleven of the nineteen had never been elected before. In other words, exactly half of the LDP incumbents and former incumbents were defeated. This high turnover rate has been a continuing characteristic of the LDP. The party has been able to rejuvenate itself and infuse new blood into its parliamentary delegation partly because of the pressures exerted by faction leaders to achieve party endorsement for their candidates and because the lower and upper house electoral systems make possible candidate turnover without changes in aggregate party strength.

The LDP and "Talent" Candidates. In the lower house elections and in the upper house local constituency elections, the LDP has consistently won a larger percentage of the total seats than of the popular vote. In the 1972 lower house election, for example, it received 46.8 percent of the popular vote but 55.1 percent of the seats (57.8 percent of the seats including the thirteen nonendorsed candidates who joined the LDP upon being elected). In the 1974 upper house local-constituency election, it won 56.6 percent of the seats with only 39.5 percent of the vote. In the national constituency, however, the party won only 35.1 percent of the seats despite a popular vote of 44.3 percent. All other parties won greater percentages of the national-constituency seats than of the vote, as indicated in Table 2-2. (Compare with figures for local constituencies in Table 1-5, p. 38.) Independents (listed as "other" in the table) also

Table 2-2

COMPARISON OF VOTE AND NUMBER OF SEATS
OBTAINED, BY PARTY, NATIONAL CONSTITUENCY,
HOUSE OF COUNCILLORS ELECTION, 1974

Party	Percentage of Seats (54 seats contested)	Percentage of National-Constituency Vote
LDP	35.1	44.3
JSP	18.5	15.2
KMT	16.7	12.1
JCP	14.8	9.4
DSP	7.4	5.9
Other	7.4	13.1

Source: Calculated from Ministry of Home Affairs data.

Table 2-3

COMPARISON OF THE VOTE OF SUCCESSFUL CANDIDATES,
BY PARTY, NATIONAL CONSTITUENCY,
HOUSE OF COUNCILLORS ELECTION, 1974

Party	Highest Winning Vote	Lowest Winning Vote	Difference
LDP	2,595,236	573,496	2,021,740
JSP	865,827	629,036	236,791
KMT	801,748	625,428	176,320
JCP	710,634	573,211	137,423
DSP	810,960	603,981	206,978

Source: Based on data from the Central Election Management Committee.

won a smaller percentage of seats than votes because of the presence
of a large number of bubble candidates and of two popular candidates who received huge vote totals.

The LDP's difficulty in gaining the maximum benefit from its
national-constituency vote is reflected in the figures in Table 2-3
which show the difference between votes obtained by the highest and
lowest winners of each party. In the case of the JCP, the gap in 1974
was 137,423 votes, for the KMT it was 176,320, and for the JSP the
figure was 236,791. But the LDP gap was over *2 million* votes. (See
also Table 1-3, p. 28.)

This tremendous difference in the votes of the LDP candidates and its poor seats/votes ratio are due largely to the drawing power of the LDP *tarento* ("talent") candidates, celebrities with national reputations and followings. In the 1974 election, the highest number of votes in the national constituency, 2,595,236, was won by a new LDP "talent," Miyata Teru, an enormously popular master of ceremonies of a folksy entertainment program on NHK, Japan's national broadcasting company. This was the third successive election in which the top vote getter had been a celebrity. In the 1968 election novelist Ishihara Shintarō won as an LDP-endorsed candidate, with over 3 million votes. In 1971 a television newscaster, JSP candidate Den Hideo, was first with 1,921,613.

Following Miyata in the 1974 national-constituency rankings, with 1,938,169 votes, was independent Ichikawa Fusae, an eighty-one-year-old former member of the upper house previously elected from the Tokyo local constituency. Ichikawa was not a television or movie type "talent," and had been defeated in the 1971 election. But in the 1974 election she gained national prominence and a vast and mostly youthful following for her almost "moneyless" campaign.

With each election the media and the opposition parties raise a hue and cry over LDP campaign excesses. In the 1974 election such criticism reached a new height. Although candidates in the national constituency were allowed by law to spend a maximum of $64,000 on their campaigns and candidates in the local constituencies an average maximum of $37,000 (the exact sum varied with the district's population), it was widely acknowledged that the limits were being grossly exceeded, particularly by LDP candidates. Although it is virtually impossible to measure what impact this criticism had on the general LDP performance in the election, there is no question but that it benefited anti-"money politics" candidates such as Ichikawa. Her protest struck a responsive chord and swept her out of what people had thought was permanent retirement back into the upper house.

Another successful protest against the exorbitant cost of campaigning was waged by a former television celebrity, forty-year-old Aoshima Yukio. Aoshima entered the campaign as an incumbent independent, having won his first election six years before. He placed third in the national-constituency contest, winning with 1,833,618 votes. His "campaign" was unique. Complaining that election campaigning in Japan required intolerable sums of money, Aoshima left for Europe the day the campaign period officially began "to study European election practices" and did not return until the voting was over. No organizational effort was conducted on his behalf but his protest gained him tremendous (and free) publicity and, in the mood that dominated the election, a far greater vote than had been expected.

Two more of the six top finishers in the 1974 election were "talents." One, Santō Akiko, was a popular, nationally known television model for Hitachi appliances, who ran with the backing of the Hitachi organization. She received 1,256,724 votes. The other, Saitō Eisaburō, was a well-known commentator on economic affairs whose articles, books, and television appearances had made him popular enough to win him over a million (1,147,951) votes.

The one JSP "talent," former television newscaster Hata Yutaka, took twelfth place with 778,728 votes. Another LDP "talent," Yamaguchi Yoshiko, a famous former movie actress and more recently the hostess of an afternoon television program ("Your 3 P.M.") popular with housewives, finished forty-sixth with 597,028 votes. The last winning "talent" candidate, in forty-eighth place with 583,886 votes, was an independent named Columbia Top. A well-known and popular comedian, Columbia Top, along with his partner Columbia Light, was noted for his political satire.

A total of eleven talent candidates ran in the 1974 national-constituency election. Seven won and four of these placed among the top six. Of the seven successful talents, four were LDP, one was JSP, and two were independents. Aoshima was the only incumbent "talent" candidate to win. "Talent" candidates took 18 percent of the total national-constituency vote. The four successful LDP "talent" candidates took exactly one-third of the total vote of the nineteen winning LDP national-constituency candidates and nearly one-fourth of all LDP national-constituency votes, as indicated in Table 2-4. In 1968 LDP "talent" candidates accounted for 15.6 percent of the LDP vote and in 1971 for 16.9 percent. The 24 percent figure in the 1974 election was thus an all-time high.

"Talent" candidates have become successful politicians in the United States and elsewhere but there probably is no country where television and movie personalities have entered elective politics in such large numbers as they have in recent years in Japan. The emergence and success of "talent" candidates in Japan do not, however, suggest some uniquely Japanese attraction toward television personalities. The reasons for their success are to be found in the particular problems of candidate selection created by the upper house election system.

The national-constituency system, in which some 53 million people voted in 1974, each choosing one name from a list of 112 candidates, presents formidable problems for campaign strategists.

Table 2-4

SHARE OF LDP VOTE RECEIVED BY LDP "TALENT" CANDIDATES, NATIONAL CONSTITUENCY, HOUSE OF COUNCILLORS ELECTION, 1974

| Candidate | Vote for LDP "Talent" Candidates | | |
	Number	As % of vote of 35 LDP candidates[a]	As % of vote of 19 winning LDP candidates[b]
Miyata Teru	2,595,236	11.12	15.42
Santō Akiko	1,256,724	5.39	7.47
Saitō Eisaburō	1,147,951	4.92	6.82
Yamaguchi Yoshiko	597,028	2.56	3.55
Total	5,596,939	23.99[c]	33.27

[a] The vote for the 35 LDP candidates was 23,332,883.

[b] The vote for the 19 winning candidates was 16,823,779.

[c] If the votes of the two unsuccessful LDP talent candidates, girls' volleyball coach Daimatsu Hirobumi (226,344) and movie producer Takechi Tetsuji (30,220) are added, the percentage of the total LDP vote obtained by "talent" candidates becomes 25.09.

Source: Calculated from the statistics of the Ministry of Home Affairs.

A candidate needs to poll somewhere around 600,000 votes to be successful and political parties have had to run candidates who have either broad backing from large organizations such as labor unions or enormous personal national recognition and popularity. Given the restrictions on candidate use of the media in Japan, "talent" candidates are unique in having been able to utilize the media to create an image appealing to a mass electorate. A candidate cannot buy time on television or on radio or advertising space in the newspapers.[7] He is not permitted to print or distribute any written materials beyond a legally prescribed number of posters and postcards.[8] Since he enters the

---

[7] Specifically, each candidate is allowed four-and-a-half minutes of television time twice during the campaign. In addition, a biographical statement can be read on radio five times and on television immediately preceding his appearance. Candidates in the national constituency are permitted to run six newspaper ads of specified length; candidates in the local constituencies are allowed five. All expenses incurred for newspaper, radio, and television advertising are paid by the government.

[8] National-constituency candidates are allowed 100,000 posters of prescribed size. They are restricted in the number of posters they can use in any one prefecture: for prefectures that comprise one lower house district, candidates can post 12,000 posters; in prefectures that make up two lower house districts, 17,000 posters are allowed; candidates can use an additional 5,000 posters for

campaign with a national reputation already established, the celebrity has clear advantages in a system where the support of a great number of voters must be mobilized and where such severe legal restrictions on campaigning prevail.

Beyond this, the significance of "talent" candidates is limited. First, "talent" is an umbrella term that conceals more than it reveals. To emphasize the number of "talent" candidates is to impose, implicitly at least, a false uniformity on the disparate individuals who fall within this category. "Talent" candidates range from informed public affairs commentators to politically innocent movie stars who seem to have first thought seriously about politics when asked to stand as party candidates.

Second, the "talent" phenomenon is limited almost entirely to the national constituency of the upper house. On the few occasions when "talent" candidates have entered lower house contests, they have done so after having first served an "apprenticeship" in the national constituency and having gained, in effect, new reputations as politicians.

Third, the number of "talent" candidates running in the national constituency is relatively small. In the 1974 election, of eighty serious national-constituency candidates (that is, excluding the bubble candidates), only eleven were "talent" candidates. Celebrities, in short, are not taking over the upper house.

Finally, "talent" candidates appear to have had difficulty in getting reelected, although the "talent boom" is still too young for any definite trends to be discernible in this regard. A few "talent" candidates, such as Ishihara Shintarō in the LDP or Den Hideo in the JSP, have demonstrated political skill and even have become important figures in their parties. But electoral success draws the "talent" candidates out of the celebrity careers that brought them popularity in the first place. After six years as backbenchers in the upper house, celebrities who are not able to establish new reputations tend to receive decidedly cool receptions from the public when they stand for reelection.

The "talent" phenomenon is largely an LDP phenomenon which has grown in importance as LDP concern over the party's steadily

---

each additional lower house district in a prefecture but cannot use more than 100,000 in total. Each poster must carry a government stamp. In the local constituency, candidates must place posters on official government poster boards. The number of such boards differs by prefecture. Each candidate may send out a limited number of campaign postcards postage free. No other printed materials can legally be distributed.

declining popular support has increased. The LDP has turned to "talent" candidates as one way to appeal to the "floating" voter, and available survey data suggest that it has correctly judged that "talent" candidates can draw the support of non-LDP voters. One poll indicated that upwards of 30 percent of the voters who expressed no party preference in the 1974 election supported "talent" candidates.[9]

On the other hand, many Japanese react negatively when questioned about the principle of celebrities running for public office. One poll conducted just before the 1974 election found that 45.5 percent of those polled disapproved of people running for the Diet "who are celebrities because of their activities in mass media such as newspapers, television and radio." Only 6 percent approved.[10] If the LDP should run many more celebrity candidates, and if the electorate should react negatively, the party's losses would be obvious. If, on the other hand, voters kept voting for celebrity candidates in large numbers while popular support for the party as a whole continued to decline, their victories would come increasingly at the expense of other LDP candidates.

Using "talent" candidates to stem the erosion of LDP strength is a stopgap measure that has created its own problems, not the least of which is the undercutting of the morale of party regulars who see their own chances of election lessened by these political amateurs who have never worked for the party. The "talent" vote cannot be influenced much by party strategy. These candidates are, in a basic sense, beyond organization. Their personal appeal is both a temptation and a danger for the LDP and for other parties looking for "talent" to boost their popular support.

The LDP and Interest Group Candidates. In addition to its "talent" candidates, the LDP runs a large number of candidates who are either representatives of large national (and LDP-supporting) organizations, or former bureaucrats with various associations behind them and with their old ministerial connections. As a result, a considerable number of upper house members elected in the national constituency represent specific organizations—labor unions in the case of the Socialists and a variety of associations in the case of the LDP. Many of these interest group candidates combine, in American terms, the roles of legislator and lobbyist.

---

[9] *Asahi Shimbun,* 28 June 1974.

[10] *Yomiuri Shimbun,* 1 July 1974 (compare with post-election poll on this subject in Passin, p. 26).

Twelve of the nineteen successful 1974 LDP candidates ran as organizational candidates.[11] Eight were former officials in the national bureaucracy who ran with the backing of a variety of groups including tobacco growers, construction industry organizations, karate clubs, sake dealers, and religious groups. Another four were representatives of special interest organizations such as the Japan Medical Association, the Bereaved Families Association, and the Association of Bicycle Manufacturers. Only two successful LDP national-constituency candidates were businessmen. A large number of LDP candidates held one position or another in business firms but except for Morishita Tai, the president of a major pharmaceutical company, and Itoyama Eitarō, an extremely wealthy businessman, LDP candidates came primarily from careers as professional politicians, government bureaucrats, *tarento* stars, or representatives of national organizations. Itoyama was, at the age of thirty-two, the youngest candidate in the election (the minimum age for candidates for the upper house is thirty) and was to gain notoriety in the election's aftermath for having more of his campaigners arrested for election law violations than any other candidate in recent memory.

Big Business and the LDP Campaign. Big business has traditionally supported the LDP by making financial contributions to the party and to leaders of party factions. But businessmen have not often stood for public office in postwar Japan and overt business support for particular candidates has been limited. In the 1974 election, however, there was an unprecedented drive by the LDP to persuade companies to sponsor individual candidates in the national-constituency election. A number of "enterprise candidates" appeared who were generously endowed with campaign funds and the support of some of Japan's most powerful corporate groups. Japanese commentators quickly coined a phrase to describe this new phenomenon—*kigyō gurumi*—which, though difficult to translate, has the approximate meaning of "depending on the enterprise for everything" (that is, for money, organization, and votes). The LDP's enterprise candidates and their lavish use of funds helped turn the conduct of the campaign itself into an important election issue.

In the spring of 1973, LDP leaders approached leading members of the big business community to discuss the possibility of running a number of well-known business figures in the coming upper house election as LDP-endorsed candidates. Their requests were received

---

[11] All LDP bureaucratic and organizational candidates and their major sources of political support are listed in Tables A-7 and A-8 in the Appendix.

coolly, with most of the businessmen consulted arguing that business should restrict its role to making financial contributions to the party.

As the election drew nearer and speculation grew about the possibility that the LDP would lose its upper house majority, party leaders again solicited business cooperation. This time, in the summer of 1973, LDP Secretary General Hashimoto Tomisaburō suggested that corporate groups sponsor the campaigns of candidates to be delegated to them by the LDP. Many corporations rejected Hashimoto's suggestion and others agreed to provide only nominal support, but two corporate groups responded enthusiastically to the LDP appeal. The Hitachi Group took on the campaign of its popular television model Santō Akiko, and the Mitsubishi Group sponsored the campaign of Saka Ken, a little-known former bureaucrat, one-time police officer, and since 1970 a counsellor to the youth department in the Prime Minister's Office.

The Mitsubishi effort on behalf of Saka Ken was directed by Mitsubishi Electric and its chairman of the board, Okubo Ken. Mitsubishi Electric has some 50,000 employees and 4,000 stores throughout the country. Unlike some Mitsubishi executives who balked at direct involvement in the campaign, fearing an anti-Mitsubishi public reaction, Okubo was enthusiastic about a direct campaign role for Mitsubishi. He dismissed criticism of his plans inside Mitsubishi, saying that "people who talk like that are not part of the Mitsubishi elite. They are big fools. Just think what would happen if there were a reversal between the conservatives and the progressives and the Communist party got free use of the Self-Defense Forces and the police." [12]

Candidate Saka was as unknown to Mitsubishi executives as to the public. But for Okubo, anonymity was no obstacle to electoral success. "Some people said that the candidate was not good enough for Mitsubishi to shoulder, but having met him in person, I know he is a fine youth [Saka was forty-six]. Since Mitsubishi is supporting him, he does not have to be widely known." [13]

Under Okubo's enthusiastic leadership, the Mitsubishi Group began about a year before the election to establish a supporters' organization (kōenkai) for Saka. The supporters' organization was staffed entirely by Mitsubishi management personnel. Okubo became president of the kōenkai and the chairmen of the board, presidents, and vice-presidents of several Mitsubishi Group companies served as kōenkai advisors. Twenty-seven Mitsubishi executives at the

---

[12] *Asahi Shimbun*, 13 June 1974.
[13] Ibid.

managing-director level were appointed directors of the *kōenkai* and thirty-nine management personnel at the division-chief level were named *kōenkai* managers. Under these leaders were middle-level Mitsubishi executives and owners of local Mitsubishi retail stores who staffed local *kōenkai* branches established throughout the country. By the time of the election 1,200,000 people had been registered as official members of the Saka Ken Kōenkai.[14]

Mitsubishi's campaign to recruit *kōenkai* members was unprecedented in scale. To recruit over a million people in slightly under a year required an extraordinary mobilization of human and financial resources. To reach its target, Mitsubishi had to go outside its own organization to recruit relatives, friends, and acquaintances of Mitsubishi employees.

In April 1974, a friend of the author living in Kobe, whom we will call Mr. Yamada, received a printed postcard from a local Mitsubishi middle-management employee, an acquaintance whom he had not seen for a number of years. The sender had stamped his seal on the card, but the printed message was from the Saka Ken Kōenkai inviting the recipient to join the supporters' organization. There was a brief biography of Saka and a message, which stated in part: "all of us in the Mitsubishi Group are expending the full energies of all Mitsubishi companies in supporting the political activities of Mr. Saka Ken and we are earnestly engaged in recruiting members for the 'Saka Ken Kōenkai.'" The card then asked the recipient to become a member, assuring him that "there will be no membership fees or other burden." The message concluded with a promise to send further material about Saka in the near future. Along with the printed message, the sender of the card penned in longhand how eager he was to be in touch again with Mr. Yamada and how much he hoped he would help him out by joining the organization.

Impressed that his acquaintance had gone to the trouble to write him while no one campaigning for any other candidate had been so solicitous, and that Saka, who had the backing of such a powerful and prestigious organization, was obviously serious about getting into the Diet, Mr. Yamada elected to join the *kōenkai*. The decision was relatively easy since it involved nothing more than having his name inscribed on the organizational rolls and receiving a continuous flow of printed materials.

Following his enrollment in the supporters' organization, Mr. Yamada received a packet of materials from the organization's headquarters. Enclosed was a printed letter thanking him for joining and

---

[14] *Nihon Keizai Shimbun*, 4 May 1974.

imploring him to "build up further the groundswell beneath Saka Ken by seeking the support of family, relatives and friends." With the letter was a tabloid-sized, full-color, four-page issue of the Saka Ken Kōenkai News, printed on heavy, glossy paper. This was the fifth such publication of the *kōenkai*. It contained a detailed history of Saka's career, messages of endorsement from leading LDP politicians, and pictures of Saka at all ages, surrounded by children and with his family.

This process was repeated not merely thousands but over a million times. Apart from the other disturbing aspects of the Mitsubishi campaign, the staggering cost of the operation became a subject of public controversy and criticism. Okubo himself remarked that "even to send just one letter to each of the 1,200,000 *kōenkai* members costs a hundred million yen (about $357,000). That is why we are distributing materials through the Mitsubishi organization, sending them in a bundle to a cooperating plant president and from him to his section chiefs and workers. Don't ask me how much it all costs!" [15]

In addition to public criticism of the extravagant sums being thrown into the campaign, rumors began to fly about unethical and possibly illegal attempts by Mitsubishi executives to coerce employees to support Saka and to recruit *kōenkai* members. Suits were brought against Mitsubishi Electric for having engaged in illegal campaign practices, one alleging, for example, that company officials in Nagoya had forced factory workers to work in the local Saka campaign office.[16] The media assault on the LDP *kigyō gurumi* election intensified and on 3 July, less than a week before the election, a bombshell exploded. Chairman Horigome Masamichi of the Central Election Management Committee, an organ established by the Ministry of Home Affairs principally to oversee the procedural aspects of the campaign, issued a statement warning the LDP and its supporting business firms that activities of companies mobilizing support for particular candidates among employees and subcontractors might violate the election law and the freedom of thought provisions of the constitution. The statement did not accuse anyone specifically of having violated the law but it expressed alarm at the way the situation was developing and called on all involved in the campaign to act with decency and in good conscience.

The "Horigome statement" made front-page headlines. Horigome's unprecedented move surprised everyone, including the other

---

[15] *Asahi Shimbun*, 18 June 1974.
[16] Ibid., 4 July 1974.

members of his election committee. Horigome had not assembled the committee to discuss the matter and had issued his statement in his individual capacity. The fact that Horigome was a vice-director of the JSP policy affairs committee brought a quick LDP counterattack that his remarks had been politically motivated. On 5 July the LDP filed suit in Tokyo District Court against Horigome for obstructing the free conduct of a campaign.

Home Ministry officials were furious at Horigome's action. The newspapers criticized him for having neglected to discuss the issue with the committee before issuing the statement. But newspaper editorials agreed that the campaign situation had warranted some kind of action. Coming so soon before the election, the Horigome statement heightened anti-LDP sentiments that had been building up against the party's campaign tactics and was probably responsible for dealing the final blow to Mitsubishi's hopes for Saka Ken. Saka was defeated in the election and returned to the obscurity he had known before Mitsubishi tried to package and sell him to the Japanese public.

While Mitsubishi's campaign for Saka was the most extravagant and widely publicized, Hitachi's effort on Santō's behalf was apparently the most effective. There are about 100 companies in the Hitachi Group, with over 30,000 management personnel on the section-chief level or above.[17] As the campaign period approached, Hitachi established a *kōenkai* called the "Hitachi Friends of Santō" and set a goal of mobilizing 600,000 votes for Santō, about twenty votes per management worker. Reports appeared in the press of Hitachi executives' pressuring owners of retail outlets, subcontractors, and employees to support Santō,[18] but the Hitachi campaign never became as controversial as that organized by Mitsubishi. It had not sought to mobilize a million votes for an unknown candidate as Mitsubishi had tried to do, but to rally Hitachi support for a well-known and popular candidate. In the end, Santō won with the fifth highest number of votes in the election, over one and a quarter million.

Prime Minister Tanaka, LDP Secretary General Hashimoto, and Mitsubishi and other business executives defended their corporate campaigns as being analogous to the Socialists' labor-union-backed campaigns. If the JSP could run a "labor union *gurumi*" campaign, they argued, why should the LDP be attacked for turning to its big business constituency for support?

---

[17] Ibid., 20 June 1974.
[18] Ibid., 21 June 1974.

Critics of the corporate campaigns responded that the issue posed by the *kigyō gurumi* effort was not that the LDP had solicited funds or had sought to rally management actively behind the LDP (although the opposition parties attacked the LDP on this score as well), but that the LDP was attempting to mobilize top executives of mammoth business enterprises to manipulate the entire corporate structure—from top to bottom—to elect particular party candidates. Company employees were not involved in the decision—as, in theory, labor union members are involved in determining union policy—and small subcontractors dependent on these powerful companies for their survival had little choice but to join the campaign effort. Critics maintained that the well-coordinated and unrestrained mobilization of the vast resources of Japanese conglomerates behind individual candidates would introduce financial and organizational power so overwhelming as to make a mockery of the idea that elections were to be freely and fairly contested.

But the fears that the corporate campaign would make a charade of the electoral process were belied by the election's results. The one "pure" *kigyō gurumi* candidate, Saka Ken, was defeated, as were two other "enterprise" candidates—Nagano Chinyū, backed by New Japan Steel, and Daimatsu Hirobumi, who ran with the support of Idemitsu Petroleum. The enterprise candidates who were successful were those who had "talent" along with business backing—candidates such as Saitō Eisaburō, who had the support of Shiseidō and other cosmetic firms.

Nonetheless, the LDP corporate campaign represented to some a disquieting development in Japan's election politics. It reflected growing LDP anxiety over the party's eroding popular support and LDP willingness to go beyond the bounds of previously accepted campaign behavior to maintain electoral strength. Although the LDP is unlikely to attempt to mobilize corporate support in quite the same manner in future elections, the *kigyō gurumi* episode does reveal the tensions present in the political process as Japan moves from a one-party-dominant to a more highly competitive party system.

Candidate Endorsement in the Local Constituencies

The forty-seven local constituencies elect from one to four members each, together electing 76 of 152 upper house members every three years for six-year terms. Many of the problems of candidate endorsement and campaign organization in the multimember local districts parallel those faced in lower house elections where seats are also determined by a single-entry ballot, multimember districting system. The problems include the possibility of candidates of the same party running in the same district and defeating each other if the vote is not distributed properly, the ability of a small party to squeeze in a candidate in a three- or four-member district, and the system's destructive effect on political party organization in a district where a party runs more than one candidate. The author has discussed these points in detail elsewhere.[19] Accordingly, they are bypassed here in favor of other aspects of the 1974 campaign in each of the three types of local-constituency district, the single-member districts, the two-member districts and the multimember districts electing three or four members.

The Metropolitan Multiparty System. The northern island of Hokkaido and the Tokyo metropolis each elect four members, and Aichi, Osaka, Hyogo, and Fukuoka elect three members each in the upper house local-constituency election. These six districts, which together elect twenty members of the upper house, most vividly reflect the multiparty system that now prevails in urban Japan. No single party dominates these districts. All the seats won by the JCP, KMT, and DSP in the 1974 local-constituency election were in these six constituencies. The performance of the various parties in the metropolitan districts in 1974 is illustrated in Table 2-5.

The emergence of a multiparty system in metropolitan Japan has forced the LDP to follow a cautious and defensive endorsement strategy in the three- and four-member districts. As its popular vote has declined, it has reduced its number of candidates to avoid having multiple candidacies turn into multiple defeats. In 1968 the LDP ran two candidates in five of these six districts. In 1974, however, it endorsed only one candidate in four of these multimember constituencies and ran two candidates only in Fukuoka and Hokkaido. The party was successful in those districts where it ran only one candidate, but in Fukuoka one of the two LDP candidates was defeated and in Hokkaido both LDP candidates lost.

The Hokkaido campaign illustrates some of the hazards of a multimember single-entry ballot system. With the 1974 election approaching, the Seirankai, a right-wing group of younger LDP members, demanded that the party endorse three candidates as it had in 1971 in order that the group's own choice—a prefectural assemblyman from Hokkaido—could have party backing to run with the two

---

[19] Gerald L. Curtis, *Election Campaigning Japanese Style* (New York: Columbia University Press, 1971).

Table 2-5

PERCENTAGE OF VOTE AND SEATS WON IN THE
SIX METROPOLITAN DISTRICTS,[a] BY PARTY,
HOUSE OF COUNCILLORS ELECTION, 1974

Party	Percent of Vote	Percent of Seats Won in 1974	Percent of Total Seats Held (seats won in 1971 and 1974)
LDP	27.17	25.0	35.0
JSP	21.81	25.0	27.5
KMT	17.93	25.0	17.5
JCP	16.40	20.0	12.5
DSP	9.71	5.0	7.5
Other	6.98	0.0	0.0
Total	100.00	100.0	100.0

[a] Three- and four-member districts.
Sources: Based on Ministry of Home Affairs and Central Election Management Committee data.

incumbents. Under pressure from the incumbents and doubtful of winning three seats, party leaders refused. Undeterred, the Seirankai candidate (Takahashi Tatsuo) ran as an independent. The Seirankai leader promoting Takahashi's candidacy was one of Hokkaido's most powerful LDP politicians and the party organization split into three groups, each supporting one of the three conservative candidates. Together the three received about 40 percent of the popular vote and polled over 200,000 more votes than the two LDP incumbent candidates had received in 1968 (1,040,747 in 1974 against 840,209 votes in 1968).[20] But they all lost. Not one of them obtained as many votes as the KMT, the JCP, or either of the JSP candidates.

The LDP Effort in the Two-Member Districts. If the three- and four-member districts have a multiparty system, the two-member local-constituency districts have a two-party system. Of the thirty candidates elected in the fifteen two-member districts in the previous election in 1971, fourteen were JSP and sixteen were LDP. The LDP

[20] The percentage of the vote obtained by the two LDP and one independent candidates, however, was less than that of the two LDP candidates in the 1968 election (39.2 percent for all three in 1974 as against 42.3 percent for the two candidates in 1968). The contrast is even more striking with the 1971 election when three LDP candidates received 48.6 percent of the vote.

won both seats in only one district, while the JSP elected fourteen of its twenty-eight successful local-constituency candidates in these two-member constituencies. Six of these fourteen outpolled the LDP candidate to win with the highest vote in their districts.

In 1968 the LDP had won both seats in seven of these two-member districts. Prime Minister Tanaka and the party leadership went into the 1974 campaign determined to recapture LDP control of these seven districts and to expand its dominance to other constituencies as well. Except for Kanagawa and Kyoto, urban districts where the LDP had no hope of winning more than one seat, the party endorsed two candidates for each of the remaining thirteen two-member districts.

To elect both its candidates in these prefecture-wide election districts, the LDP endorsed notable prefectural politicians—governors and former governors, long-time prefectural assemblymen, and others influential in local politics. Several LDP incumbents who had won in 1968 decided not to stand for reelection in 1974, leaving just two districts (Fukushima and Kumamoto) where both candidates were incumbents. There were three districts (Nagano, Okayama and Kagoshima) where neither candidate was an incumbent.

The occupational backgrounds of the thirteen nonincumbent LDP candidates suggest the extent of the party's reliance on local politicians for the 1974 election. Three were governors who retired to run in the election. In Prime Minister Tanaka's home prefecture of Niigata, for example, the incumbent candidate was a former governor of the prefecture and the other candidate, a close Tanaka ally in Niigata politics, was the incumbent governor. In Ibaragi Prefecture, one candidate was a governor's wife running as a conservative independent. Five of the nonincumbent LDP candidates were prefectural assemblymen, several of whom had served as speakers or vice-speakers of their assemblies. One was the mayor of the largest city in Nagano Prefecture. The other three included a local Chamber of Commerce executive and two former bureaucrats, one from the national tax office and the other from the agriculture division of a prefectural government. Many of the LDP's lower house representatives and upper house members elected from prefectural constituencies had in the past been local politicians but the party had never made as concerted an effort to bring active local politicians into a national election as it did in 1974.

The LDP leaders concentrated their attention on these two-member constituencies during the campaign, with Tanaka and other top party officials visiting these districts frequently. An intense effort was made to publicize the candidates and get out the vote. It was Tanaka's confidence that the party would dominate the two-member districts that led to his prediction that the LDP would take seventy-five seats in the election.

Two assumptions underlay the LDP's optimistic belief that it could monopolize many of the two-member districts. The first was that its candidates, with their strong personal organizations, local recognition, and prestige, when supported by a vigorous campaign by the party on their behalf, would substantially raise the LDP vote. The second was that the JCP and the KMT would draw considerable support away from the JSP, enabling the paired LDP candidates to win. The JCP, as in the past, was planning to run one candidate in each of the two-member districts. The KMT was going to enter this arena for the first time, running candidates in thirteen of these districts. KMT and JCP candidates were serious contenders for seats only in the Kyoto and Kanagawa constituencies. In the other districts only the JSP was capable of challenging the LDP.

In 1971 the LDP received 49.3 percent of the vote in the two-member constituencies, the JSP 35.8 percent, the JCP 11.6 percent, and the DSP and minor nonparty candidates the remaining 3.3 percent. The KMT ran no candidates in these districts. With KMT candidates entered in thirteen of these districts in the 1974 election (the exceptions being Fukushima and Kumamoto, with the KMT supporting the JSP candidate in the latter district) and with the expected rise in popular support for the JCP, many observers—party officials and media commentators alike—predicted that KMT and JCP candidates would drain votes from the JSP, allowing the LDP to capture both seats in several of these districts.

However, in the election the LDP won both seats only in Kumamoto, ironically the only two-member district where the JSP and KMT cooperated in supporting the same candidate. In several cases the new LDP candidate won, displacing the LDP incumbent.[21] One of the biggest personal embarrassments for Tanaka was that he was unable to realize his goal even in his own home prefecture of Niigata. Not only did the voters reject one of the two LDP candidates in Niigata, they rejected the one closest politically to the prime minister. The LDP percentage of the 1974 vote in the two-member districts declined by a small but nonetheless significant amount (3 percent) in spite of the party's attempts to increase its vote. More significant, perhaps, is a comparison of the 1974 results with the LDP vote in the 1968 election when LDP members of the upper house whose terms were

---

[21] For more information, see Blaker in this volume, pp. 95-96 and 112-115.

expiring in 1974 were elected. In 1968 the LDP received 53.8 percent of the vote, 7.5 percent more than in 1974, as indicated in Table 2-6. In 1974 the only sizable gains in these districts were scored by the KMT, which went from zero in 1971 to 11.3 percent of the vote in 1974. The JCP, with 11.6 percent of the 1971 vote, received only 9.0 percent of the 1974 vote. The JSP vote declined markedly, down 7.5 percentage points from 1971, to 28.2 percent. Comparisons of party performance in 1971 and 1974 are shown in Table 2-7. Although the JSP loss in popular support was substantial, support for the KMT was not large enough to reduce the JSP vote to a level where both the LDP candidates, unable to divide the vote equally between themselves, could outpoll the JSP candidate.

For at least the next two upper house elections the two-member constituencies are likely to continue to be dominated by the LDP and

Table 2-6
LDP PERCENTAGE OF THE VOTE, TWO-MEMBER LOCAL-CONSTITUENCY DISTRICTS, HOUSE OF COUNCILLORS ELECTIONS, 1968, 1971, AND 1974

	1968	1971	1974
Fukushima	63.4	57.5	52.1
Ibaragi	53.0	65.7	51.6[a]
Tochigi	54.6	53.9	56.0[a]
Gumma	67.3	51.9	52.2
Saitama	56.2	44.3	42.0
Chiba	49.2	42.7	42.8
Kanagawa	37.9	42.7	25.9
Niigata	60.6[a]	48.0	58.2
Nagano	35.1	40.4	41.2
Shizuoka	63.6	59.6	49.0
Kyoto	32.9	36.2	37.2
Okayama	62.6	40.0	50.9
Hiroshima	48.2	51.1	53.3
Kumamoto	73.1	66.7	65.4
Kagoshima	69.5	53.2	59.5
Overall	53.8	49.3	46.3

[a] Includes vote for LDP candidates and for conservative-related independents.
Sources: Calculations for 1968 and 1971 are adapted from data in Nishihira Shigeki, *Nihon no senkyo* (Tokyo: Shiseidō, 1972), pp. 426-472; 1974 figures are based on statistics from the Central Election Management Committee.

Table 2-7

PERCENTAGE OF VOTE, TWO-MEMBER LOCAL-CONSTITUENCY DISTRICTS, BY PARTY, HOUSE OF COUNCILLORS ELECTIONS, 1971 AND 1974

| Party | Percentage of Total Vote | | Difference |
	1971	1974	
LDP[a]	49.32	46.33	− 2.99
JSP	35.78	28.24	− 7.54
KMT	-0-	11.25	+ 11.25
JCP	11.56	9.00	− 2.56
DSP	1.00	2.54	+ 1.54
Other	2.34	2.64	+ .30
	100.00	100.00	

[a] Votes for winning conservative-related independent candidates are included in LDP totals.

Sources: Based on data in Nishihira, *Nihon no senkyo*, pp. 426-472, and on Central Election Management Committee statistics.

the JSP. The LDP, expecting further erosion of its popular support, is likely to cut back to one the number of candidates it runs in many two-member districts. The party will have little difficulty electing a single candidate in most of these districts. The JSP also is in a fairly comfortable position in these constituencies, even though its support is declining faster than that for any other party. Neither the KMT nor the JCP is likely to present a real challenge for several years to come.[22]

One-Party Dominance in Single-Member Districts. Although one-party dominance has ended in the two-, three-, and four-member districts in the upper house local constituency, it remains the pattern in the primarily rural areas that comprise the twenty-six single-member districts. In the 1974 election the LDP won in twenty-four of these districts.[23]

The LDP vote was a little higher in the single-member constituencies than in the two-member districts but it yielded a disproportion-ately higher number of seats. LDP dominance in these districts

[22] See Blaker, pp. 110-112.

[23] The exceptions were Tokushima, where the LDP incumbent ran as an independent, won, and later rejoined the party, and Okinawa, where the LDP candidate lost to a popular independent who ran with the backing of all the opposition parties.

continues in spite of a decline in popular support for the party. The LDP received a majority of the vote in fourteen of these twenty-six districts in 1974, compared to sixteen in 1971. It obtained over 60 percent of the 1968 vote in four districts, but in 1974 only one district gave the party more than 60 percent of the vote. Even in the twelve districts where its vote did not exceed 50 percent in 1974 (with the exception of Okinawa), the LDP won because of the competition among the opposition parties. In the 1971 election the opposition had demonstrated that it could combine to defeat the LDP in single-member constituencies: KMT and DSP support for JSP candidates resulted in JSP victories in eight of these districts. But in the absence of opposition cooperation the LDP is likely to continue to dominate the single-member constituencies.

LDP dominance in single-member constituencies, much like Democratic dominance in some southern congressional districts in the United States, means that often the most vigorously contested battle is for the party's endorsement. Japan, however, does not have a system of primary elections: endorsement is determined by the party itself and the party rules and party practice provide important roles for both the prefectural party chapter and the national party leadership. Members of the prefectural chapter—heads of city, town, and village branches, representatives of the local party's women and youth sections, and chapter executives—determine the chapter's recommendations for endorsement, which are usually made by formal ballot of the membership if there is more than one contender for the nomination. These recommendations are forwarded to Tokyo and the national party leadership makes the final decision on candidate endorsement. Chapter recommendations occasionally are rejected or modified, particularly in lower house elections, either because the chapter recommends more candidates than the leadership feels it is safe to run in these multimember districts or because factional pressures at the top force the endorsement of more candidates than the chapter wants to run. In principle, any incumbent desiring to run is given the party endorsement as a matter of course unless he has seriously violated party rules. In upper house single-member districts, however, there is rarely any controversy over the chapter's recommendation. Only one candidate can be endorsed and the primacy of the prefectural chapter in deciding which individual should receive the party's nomination is generally recognized.

In the 1974 election, however, a major intra-LDP controversy emerged over the endorsement of a candidate in the Tokushima single-member district. The manner in which the LDP candidate was chosen and the extensive corruption evident in the campaign received widespread media attention and became something of a national scandal. It quickly escalated into a conflict between Prime Minister Tanaka and the man who was eventually to succeed him in that office, Miki Takeo.

In the 1968 election Kujime Kentarō, an executive of the prefecture's farmers' association and a colleague of the prefecture's most illustrious politician, Miki Takeo, ran as the LDP candidate and was elected to the upper house. He served without particular distinction but without violating any party rules and, as the 1974 election approached, he prepared to run again. Much to Kujime's dismay, however, an unsuccessful candidate in the 1972 lower house election in Tokushima—Gotōda Masaharu—declared his intention to fight Kujime for the party's nomination. Gotōda entered the fray with impressive backing. A former high official in the Police Agency and close confidant of Prime Minister Tanaka, Gotōda had devoted his time after his 1972 election defeat to cultivating support among the members of the party's prefectural chapter. Gotōda missed few opportunities to demonstrate to the local politicians his close relationship with the prime minister and they began coming in increasing numbers to support his candidacy. The issue finally was confronted in the Tokushima LDP chapter. Without going into the details of the fight for the chapter's recommendation, we can say that the situation rapidly deteriorated into an extraordinary effort by both camps to secure support. Allegations of political pressure from Tokyo and of the bribing of local politicians reached such a pitch that the president of the chapter moved up the date of the meeting in which the chapter's recommendation was to be decided in order to prevent the situation from becoming even worse than it had become.

At the meeting members voted by secret ballot, but after the ballots had been counted the chapter leadership refused to announce the results. In an unprecedented action, it put the ballots back in the ballot box and took it to Tokyo. There it remained for three months in the safe in the office of the vice-president of the LDP. In September 1973 the ballots were counted again and Gotōda was declared the recommended candidate of the Tokushima LDP chapter. Tanaka accepted the Tokushima recommendation, efforts by Miki to have the party reverse the decision failed, and Gotōda launched his campaign as the official LDP-endorsed candidate.

Gotōda's endorsement threatened not only Kujime's political future but Miki's reputation as well. The decision was made to have Kujime run as an independent. Miki faction Diet members from around the country, as well as other incumbent Diet members who feared that the precedent established in Tokushima could lead to the dumping of incumbent members of the Diet elsewhere, traveled to Tokushima to campaign for Kujime. Tanaka, for his part, visited the prefecture to lend his support to the Gotōda effort. The campaign itself degenerated into one of the dirtiest in a national election in recent memory. Miki asserted at one point that he had not seen a campaign as filthy as the one being conducted by the LDP in Tokushima since the campaigns of government-sponsored candidates during the wartime period.

In the end the independent Kujime emerged as the winner. Although local observers thought the race would be close, he defeated Gotōda by a substantial margin, a consequence probably of his being the beneficiary of a considerable "sympathy vote" (dōjōhyō) and of a voter reaction against the tactics employed by the supporters of the LDP candidate in this politically conservative prefecture.

Conclusion

Despite widespread criticism of LDP campaign practices, the party came out of the election with only a small decline in its popular vote and with a small majority of seats in the upper house. The parties of the "progressive camp" seemed intent on making electoral gains at each other's expense. Their vigorous competition for the anti-LDP vote undercut whatever hopes they may have had for bringing about a "reversal of the conservatives and the progressives."

On the other hand, the LDP was unable to reverse the trend of declining popular support for the party despite its strenuous efforts to do so. Its "enterprise" and "talent" candidates, its use of large sums of money in the campaign, and its rather crude attempt to turn the election into an "LDP-JCP confrontation" (Ji-Kyō taiketsu) reflected the frustrations and enmities within the party leadership as it contemplated the end of an era of unchallenged LDP dominance. Such tactics probably hurt the party's general performance at the polls more than they helped. The LDP vote in the local-constituency contests fell below 40 percent for the first time and the four-percentage-point drop in LDP popular support from the previous election was the largest decline in twelve years.

But the most direct consequence of the campaign was that it provided an additional weapon for anti-Tanaka forces in the LDP to attack the prime minister and to increase the pressure for his resignation. Tanaka's personal leadership of the campaign set him up as the prime target for criticism. Shortly after the close of the campaign, Miki resigned from the government and stated that he would devote his full energies to bringing about party reform. His sentiments were echoed by Fukuda Takeo, who broke with the Tanaka government shortly after Miki's departure. His break was followed by an announcement by Keidanren, the most important big business association in Japan, that it would no longer solicit funds for the LDP and that it would lend its support to efforts to bring about reform in the system of political funding. Tanaka finally was forced from office in December 1974. After a period of intense negotiations among party leaders, Miki emerged as the party's compromise candidate for party president and prime minister.

The consequences of the 1974 upper house election campaign, therefore, appear somewhat paradoxical. The LDP was subjected to intense criticism of its campaign practices but came out of the election with relatively minor losses. The opposition parties had the opportunity to obtain a majority of seats in the upper house but competed among themselves to defeat each other's candidates. The LDP appeared to swerve markedly to the right in stressing a Communist threat and in involving big business in the campaign in an unprecedented manner but then moved quickly to dump the party's leader and dissociate itself from his campaign style.

The campaign, in short, revealed some of the dynamic aspects of a party system moving out of an era of one-party dominance into a new and more complex period. Whether the LDP will remain a catch-all conservative party—pragmatic, relatively flexible, and restrained in its approach—and whether the opposition parties will be able to transform themselves from parties of protest into parties prepared to assume governmental responsibility were questions raised, but not answered, by the 1974 upper house campaign.

3

THE OUTCOME OF THE 1974 ELECTION: PATTERNS AND PERSPECTIVES

Michael K. Blaker

The Changing Electorate

The Japan that went to the polls on 7 July differed in many respects from the Japan of previous elections. Ongoing processes of intense demographic and social change—urbanization, industrialization, upward mobility, spreading affluence—had exerted a profound impact upon the shape and composition of the Japanese electorate.

Of greatest political significance, perhaps, was the growing disproportion between the size of electoral districts, their population, and their representation in the upper house. Representatives of ten districts where 52 percent of the eligible voting population lived filled only 31 percent of the local constituency seats in the House of Councillors. This imbalance between population and political representation had increased since 1971, and in Japan there is no Senate-like formula for equal representation regardless of the size of the electoral unit.

There were 75.7 million Japanese eligible to vote in the 1974 election—a rise of slightly over 4 million in just three years. Part of this increase can be readily explained: some 610,000 voters from Okinawa were participating in a House of Councillors election for the first time since the island's reversion to Japanese jurisdiction in mid-1972. More important, since the 1971 upper house contest, the population and number of eligible voters had become more concentrated in the crowded urban areas of the Kantō and Kansai regions, with the largest increases in Osaka, Hyogo, Saitama, Ibaragi, Chiba, Shizuoka, and Kanagawa prefectures. Over a million names were added to the

I would like to thank Suzanne Seear-Brown for her assistance with the statistical data used in this study.

1974 voting rolls from the three suburban prefectures surrounding the capital—Kanagawa, Saitama, and Chiba.[1]

There were significantly more eligible women voters than men, 39.1 million to 36.6 million, and voting patterns by sex show that Japanese women were taking their political responsibilities as seriously as men. A slightly higher percentage of eligible women than men have cast ballots in every national election since 1968.

The electorate was also younger than it had been three years before. One-fourth of the potential voting population was composed of Japanese in their twenties, a twelve-percentage-point increase over 1968; a third was over forty-eight, an eight-percentage-point decrease over the same period. And the electorate was better educated—college graduates constituted nearly 10 percent of the voting population and over 37 percent had completed high school (or the old middle school). Moreover, it was increasingly exposed to the mass media—radio, television, and the newspapers. The three top Japanese dailies—*Asahi*, *Yomiuri*, and *Mainichi*—rank first, second, and third worldwide in number of copies printed.

Fewer Japanese than before were engaged in farming: the percentage of the population engaged in farming had declined by thirteen percentage points from 1960 to 1972 and the number of farming households by over a million since 1955. In addition, more than half of the members of farming households worked at nonfarming jobs. While the proportion of Japanese in the primary (mining, farming, fishing) sector of the economy had fallen, that in the secondary (construction, manufacturing) and especially in the tertiary sector (transportation, communication, wholesale and retail trading and service industries) had surged ahead during the preceding decade. Further, nearly 12 million Japanese belonged to labor unions, up 4 million in ten years.[2]

Statistics showed that the Japanese were more affluent than before, but the state of the economy and double-digit inflation left few Japanese feeling prosperous. Consumer prices had climbed 25 percent from the year before, and of all the issues bothering the Japanese citizenry before the election, inflation topped the list. One opinion survey taken in June showed that four out of five Japanese believed that high prices were the central election issue, followed in order of importance by social welfare, education, pollution and the

---

[1] Based on 1971 and 1974 figures from the Ministry of Home Affairs and published in the *Asahi Shimbun*, 16 June 1974.

[2] Office of the Prime Minister, Bureau of Statistics, *Statistical Handbook of Japan* (Tokyo, 1973), pp. 29, 114-124; *Asahi Shimbun*, 12 May 1974.

quality of life, housing, taxes, transportation, agriculture, and regional development.[3] National defense and foreign policy were not subjects of urgent public interest: what occupied the public mind was butter, not guns, and matters close to home, not far away. The campaign centered on the many facets of one vital issue—the state of the economy—and each party and candidate had to address this issue in some way. None tried more conspicuously than Santō Akiko, one of three LDP women hopefuls in the national constituency, whose slogan was "let's bring politics into the kitchen."

The pulse of the Japanese electorate is probably taken more frequently than that of any other electorate, particularly before a key national election. All the major newspapers and many local newspapers, the news agencies such as Kyodo, and the television networks conduct surveys throughout the preelection campaign, with follow-up polls to gauge shifting trends. The quality of these polls varies markedly, especially in precision of questionnaire design and in sample size, but if one bears in mind their qualitative differences and uses them carefully, poll data are useful in examining two points: the consistency or inconsistency of certain public attitudes over an extended period of time, and the influence of the polls themselves upon voting behavior. Also, while one might challenge the quality or reliability of such survey data as indicators of voting performance, they are fairly accurate and provide a barometer of Japanese popular thinking about politics, political parties, and politicians.

Surveys taken in Japan in the backwash of the energy crisis and before the 1974 election showed a persisting sense of unease among the Japanese people. Polls uncovered public dissatisfaction with the political situation, anxiety about the value of the political process, and doubt that conditions would improve. Over three-fourths of a *Mainichi* sample, for instance, voiced unhappiness with the existing political state of affairs and the course of national politics.[4] Interestingly, 61 percent of the LDP supporters in this sample joined in this negative appraisal.

Much of the discontent was focused on the politicians. In the same poll, to the question "What comes to your mind when you think of Japanese politicians?" the replies used more than any others were the adjectives "rich," "tricky," "unfair," "arrogant," and "decrepit." A mere fraction (3 percent) of those polled believed that Diet members fulfill their campaign promises. In addition to this reservoir of popular dissatisfaction with politics and politicians, there was widespread

---

[3] *Mainichi Shimbun*, 17 June 1974. (Compare with Curtis in this volume, p. 47.)
[4] *Mainichi Shimbun*, 26 June 1974.

Figure 3-1

TRENDS IN PARTY SUPPORT RATES, 1959–1974

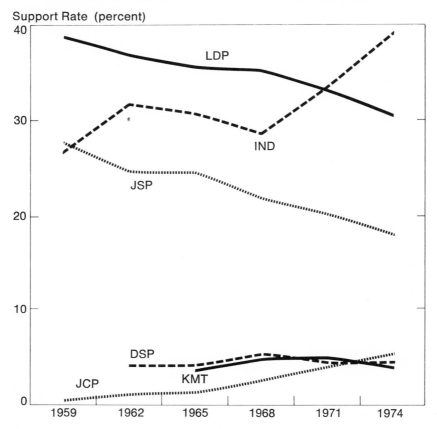

Source: Based on *Asahi Shimbun* surveys taken shortly before House of Councillors elections in these years and published one to two weeks prior to the elections.

disaffection toward the political parties, particularly the LDP and the JSP. As Figure 3-1 illustrates, this merely continued a long-term trend of eroding support for these two major parties.

LDP support rates were down slightly from their levels of three years before.[5] Poll results varied considerably: the *Asahi* measured LDP support at 30.5 percent, the *Mainichi*, 36 percent, *Jiji Tsūshin*,

[5] *Yomiuri Shimbun*, 1 July 1974, showed a support rate of 36 percent, down 2.4 percentage points from 1971; *Mainichi Shimbun*, 3 July 1974, down one percentage point to 36 percent; *Asahi Shimbun*, 26 June 1974, down 5.1 percentage points (1965-1974 period).

40 percent. But all the surveys agreed that LDP support had eroded. Moreover, then Prime Minister Tanaka's appeal had plummeted to about 20 percent of the electorate, the lowest since he had taken office in 1972.[6] Polls hinted at still another (and in its long-term implications far more serious) source of trouble for the LDP: its shrinking base of support. The LDP has been anchored in the tradition-oriented strata of Japanese society—the self-employed, those engaged in agriculture and fishing or living in nonurban areas, voters in their fifties and sixties, and the less well educated.[7] As the socioeconomic composition of the Japanese electorate has changed, with the electorate becoming more urban, better educated, and more affluent, the party's support has dwindled. According to one poll, just one person in four of those under forty years of age backed the LDP, and one in eight backed the Tanaka cabinet.[8] Labor constituted only about 15 percent of total LDP support.[9]

Thinning public support for the LDP, however, did not significantly raise support for the opposition parties. JSP popularity had also declined, off about three percentage points since the previous upper house election, to a level hovering around 20 percent. While public support for the JCP had risen slightly from 1971 to 1974, support for the KMT had declined and that for the DSP was unchanged. The opposition in any case was not the major beneficiary of lessened LDP support, nor did the public see the opposition as offering any salvation. One poll framed the question directly: "If a coalition government came to power, do you think that problems relating to prices, housing, and the environment would worsen or improve?" [10] Nearly 55 percent replied "no change." Some 62 percent of a *Sankei* newspaper-sponsored poll sample thought the political situation would stay the same no matter who won the election.[11]

Instead of generating public support for the other parties or igniting an anti-LDP protest movement, public attitudes seemed merely to swell the ranks of the disenchanted and the uncommitted, what is commonly labelled the "floating vote" (*fudōhyō*) or "unconcerned vote" (*mukanshinhyō*) or "hidden vote" (*senzaihyō*). Before the 1974 election, these uncommitted or "post-political" (*datsu-seiji*)

---

[6] *Mainichi Shimbun*, 24 percent (22 June 1974); *Yomiuri Shimbun*, 21.2 percent (1 July 1974); *Jiji Tsūshin*, 25.7 percent (25 June 1974). (See Curtis, p. 46.)

[7] *Asahi Shimbun*, 29 June 1974.

[8] *Yomiuri Shimbun*, 1 July 1974.

[9] *Asahi Shimbun*, 29 June 1974.

[10] *Yomiuri Shimbun*, 1 July 1974.

[11] *Sankei Shimbun*, 5 June 1974.

Japanese, who answer either "don't know" or "no preference" to queries about party affiliation, were estimated to include about 30 percent of the potential voting population.[12] While this figure was not much above past percentages, any increase in the uncommitted vote was bound to dim the LDP's election outlook since the floating voter has tended in past elections to favor the opposition. The floating vote, in contrast to the potential LDP vote, is composed largely of white-collar professionals and younger persons and is highest in the metropolitan areas. An *Asahi* poll taken shortly before the election pegged the Tokyo floating vote at a startling 40 percent.[13] The potential danger to the LDP from this mass of uncommitted voters is somewhat attenuated by the floater's tendency to vote less frequently than others.

Curiously, despite their hostility toward politicians and their disillusionment with the political situation, Japanese voters were not apathetic. Voter interest in the election was at an all-time high—far above its level in 1971 when only 59 percent voted. It was expected that voters would turn out in record numbers. Several 1974 surveys forecast a voting rate of 70 percent—a figure that could scarcely reflect apathy, even in a country where that word has come to mean a turnout of under 65 percent. Popular political participation by voting in national elections has become a thoroughly ingrained habit in postwar Japan.

In the months preceding the election the mood of the Japanese public was one of interest tempered by skepticism; the mood of the parties' leadership, one of anxiety heightened by a sense of crisis. In this atmosphere, with political party support waning among the public, the key issue was which party would capture the lion's share of the floating vote that was estimated by one source at 28 million.[14]

The news media dramatized the election as an epochal conservative-progressive confrontation, using the phrase *hokaku gyakuten*

---

[12] *Yomiuri Shimbun*, 1 July 1974, gives 28.5 percent; *Mainichi Shimbun*, 3 July 1974, 32 percent; *Asahi Shimbun*, 26 July 1974, 37.4 percent, the sharpest increase. For details on party support and the floating vote for the 1971 election see Tomita Nobuo, "Daikyūkai sangiin tsūjō senkyo no bunseki," *Meiji daigaku seikeironsō*, vol. 39, nos. 3-6 (March 1972), pp. 395-399.

As major reasons for being uncommitted, respondents in one poll cited, variously, "no concern with politics," "parties think only of self-interest," and "parties fail to carry out their pledges." This sense of distrust of politics and political parties was deepest among college students (74 percent in one sample) and college graduates. Thirty-seven percent of the same sample had "no interest" in the election. (*Yomiuri Shimbun*, 1 July 1974.)

[13] *Asahi Shimbun*, 26 June 1974.

[14] Ibid.

(reversal of the conservatives and the progressives): the "conservatives" (*hoshu*) were depicted as locked in mortal combat with the "progressives" (*kakushin*), with the stakes being "reversal" (*gyakuten*) of their relative strength in the House of Councillors.[15] Attempts were made to reify the phrase on television by computerized charts and graphs showing the ruling *hoshu* forces in one color and the *kakushin* challengers in another.

Such sloganeering and polar characterizations are as common in Japanese politics as they are in American. But they were not necessary to arouse public interest in the 1974 campaign, and for the election, diffuse loyalties to the "conservatives" or the "progressives" were less important than the erosion of party support and the related increase in the size of the floating vote. More voters than ever would be swayed by the individual personalities, styles, and campaign tactics of the candidates.

In practical terms, the problem common to the leaders of all the parties as they mulled over possible candidates and campaign strategies—and perhaps the central issue of the entire 1974 election campaign—was how to maintain established foundations of party loyalty while at the same time opening new avenues of support. In the local constituencies, each district presented special constraints and special opportunities for each party, but it was the competition in the fifteen two-member districts that would test the major parties most severely. In the national-constituency arena the obstacles facing party strategists were most sharply visible. It is conventional wisdom that winners in the national domain are well-known personalities or candidates backed by strong national organizations. Winning also requires boundless physical energy and money, or possibly an idealistic appeal, and some degree of luck. Even for a candidate who enjoys these assets, however, attracting votes in the national contest is—to borrow the Japanese metaphor—"like trying to catch hold of a cloud."

The candidates selected by the various parties seemed to reflect the changing composition and preferences of the Japanese electorate. There were more candidates in total (349), more women (18), more nonincumbents (70 percent), and more "talent" contenders (13) running than in any upper house contest in twenty years. Table 3-1 shows the overall distribution of candidates for the 1974 election by party and occupational background.

There were 16 percent more new candidates in the local constituencies than in 1971. Of sixty local LDP candidates only twenty-six were new, but nearly all the JCP candidates (forty-three of forty-five)

---

[15] See Curtis, p. 48.

Table 3-1

CANDIDATES BY PARTY AND OCCUPATION,
ALL CONSTITUENCIES,
HOUSE OF COUNCILLORS ELECTION, 1974[a]

Occupation	Number of Candidates						
	LDP	JSP	KMT	DSP	JCP	Other	Total
Ex-bureaucrats	29	—	—	1	—	—	30
Labor	—	26	—	5	10	2	43
"Talent"	6	1	—	1	—	5	13
Party workers	1	4	10	1	25	—	41
Prefectural governors and vice-governors	11	2	—	—	—	—	13
Prefectural assemblymen	14	15	16	2	4	4	55
Self-employed	10	5	6	2	11	4	38
Business-related	20	2	4	2	—	—	28
Other	4	2	9	—	3	4	22
Total	95	57	45	14	53	19	283

a Excludes 66 "bubble" or non-serious candidates. (See also Appendix, Table A-2.)
Sources: *Asahi Shimbun*, 16 June 1974; *Mainichi Shimbun*, 17 June, 11 July 1974; and *Sankei Shimbun*, 10 July 1974.

were running for the first time, as were those from the KMT (thirty-three of thirty-six), the DSP (eight of nine) and the JSP (thirty-eight of forty-five). Also, candidates were younger in the local constituencies than in the national constituency.

Faced with the prospect of long-term decline and a strengthened opposition, the LDP took an aggressive line for the election.[16] The party mobilized three types of candidate for the campaign. First, there were, as always, ex-bureaucrats. Nearly one-third of all LDP candidates had had experience in the upper levels of the Japanese bureaucracy. Second, particularly for the local-constituency contests, the LDP picked "OB" or "old boy" politicians, mostly incumbent or former prefectural governors and vice-governors who were well-known in their districts. Third, the LDP pinned its hopes on "talents" and "enterprise" candidates. These LDP contenders were chosen mainly for their appeal to the floating vote, nearly a third of which had gone to celebrity candidates in the previous upper house elec-

16 Described in Curtis, pp. 46-48, 65-71.

tion.[17] LDP candidates were slightly younger on the average than in past elections.[18]

The Socialists fielded fifty-seven candidates, endorsing eleven and recommending one in the national constituency and forty-four for local prefectural contests. Three-fourths of the JSP candidates had had some experience in labor unions and fifteen were prefectural assemblymen. JSP leaders tried to solidify the party's Sōhyō labor union base of support and at the same time attract nonlabor support. To expand JSP strength among the floating vote and into agricultural areas, sixteen nonlabor candidates were added to its roster of hopefuls—university professors, mayors, lawyers, and clergymen. The question, of course, was whether the workers would vote for nonlabor candidates.

The DSP, the smallest of the four opposition parties, faced an analogous problem of lessened support with Dōmei, its 2.3-million-member supporting labor organization. The JCP had scored gains in Dōmei as well as Sōhyō. Like the Socialists, the Democratic Socialists had sought to move beyond their labor union base: of nine local and five national candidates, eight were unaffiliated with Dōmei.

The Kōmeitō undertook a most ambitious base-building effort as it sought to prepare for the next general election by establishing national support beyond Sōka Gakkai, the lay Buddhist organization that had been the party's source of strength in the past. The party softened the tone of its policy line and ran more candidates than ever before—forty-five (thirty-six local and nine national). In the local constituencies, nine KMT candidates were unaffiliated with Sōka Gakkai but most were younger party workers or prefectural assemblymen with Gakkai backgrounds. Its local candidates were unknowns—thirty-one of thirty-six were running for the first time. Also unknown was the impact these candidates would have on election results in the local contests.

The KMT's assertive program was surpassed only by that of the JCP. The Communists' goal was to triple the number of seats they held in the House of Councillors. There were fifty-three JCP candidates (eight national, forty-five local). As in the past JCP candidates had been active in party organizational work, but this time there was an added twist. To build its national base and to entice more of the

---

[17] See Curtis, Table 2-4.

[18] There had been a heated intraparty debate about running elderly candidates, but the idea of not running candidates over seventy years old had been discarded. Although the party ran no one over eighty and five more candidates in their thirties, there were more septuagenarians and seven fewer in their forties than in 1971. (See Appendix, Table A-1.)

floating vote, the party selected what were called the "three *shi*"—that is *kyō-shi* (teachers), *i-shi* (doctors), and *bengo-shi* (lawyers). These numbered twenty-three, or 43 percent of all JCP candidates.

Along with seeking ways of shoring up their respective political support structures, the opposition parties spent considerable time trying to devise a workable united front formula for the election. It appeared that the sole hope for an opposition upset was their assembling an effective anti-LDP coalition. The opposition parties' hopes for victory in 1974 had originated in the 1971 election, when solidarity campaigns among the opposition had helped bring disaster to the conservatives.[19] This favorable experience in the previous election, their unified resistance to the conservatives' single-member election district reform plan, and their belief that high prices and pollution would lead voters to spurn the LDP, led to ambitious plans for cooperation in twelve or more districts in the 1974 campaign.[20] It was expected that these joint campaigns would be the key to an opposition victory. Three months before the election, however, the plans started to unravel. Apart from a JSP-JCP joint campaign in Kochi Prefecture, all cooperation was between the Socialists and Kōmeitō. The KMT was to work for JSP candidates informally in nine districts where no KMT candidate was standing and formally in Kumamoto, Toyama, and Tottori. In Wakayama the JSP would back the KMT. While the stated formula was an even-handed "*gibu ando tēku*" (from the English "give and take," and meaning the same thing), the KMT was to give far more than it was to take.

What was the chance of an opposition upset? For the fifty-four national-constituency seats there was little drama. Assuming victory for the mass organization party candidates, the JCP and KMT together would take seventeen seats. The JSP was expected to win ten of twelve, the DSP four of five, and one independent was favored. The LDP, which had never taken more than twenty-three in past elections, would take the rest—twenty-two seats.

The situation in the local constituencies was far more uncertain. Any hope of an opposition victory hinged upon the outcome in the pivotal two-member districts, six of which are in the densely populated Kantō region where LDP popular support had tumbled four percentage points in just three years.[21] Opposition cooperation and the large number of new KMT candidates further complicated the local-constituency picture. Nevertheless, the outcome seemed fairly

---

[19] For details, see Curtis, pp. 50-53.

[20] *Chōsa Geppō*, March 1974, pp. 1-16.

[21] *Asahi Shimbun*, 26 June 1974.

predictable on the eve of the election. If the LDP were to control the conservative one-member districts (as most anticipated), perform creditably in the key two-member battlegrounds (a premise many doubted), and maintain the status quo in the national constituency (a strong possibility), the party would take seventy to seventy-five seats. The expected high voting rate was believed to favor the LDP,[22] and despite the large number of undecided voters and widely publicized charges of LDP campaign violations just days before the election, it looked as if Tanaka's party, having labored mightily in a wearying campaign, had fended off any chance of an historic reversal of power.

Analysis of the Results

Despite the driving winds and drenching rains brought by the season's eighth typhoon, 73.2 percent of the eligible Japanese voters braved the elements to cast ballots on 7 July. The record voting rate—nearly nine percentage points above the postwar average for upper house elections—was bound to overturn many preelection prognoses and campaign strategies. As is usual in Japanese elections, the voting rate was lowest in the metropolitan and urban districts and highest in the rural single-member districts, even though the outcome was not in doubt in these conservative-dominated areas. In those two-member districts where the LDP was running two candidates, the voting rate soared to 78.5 percent. It was clear that LDP strategists had correctly predicted that two LDP contenders in a two-member district would generate voter interest. But whether the heavy turnout would produce a richer harvest of LDP votes would be the test of their campaign's effectiveness. The results of the 1974 election are given in Table 3-2.[23]

As the results came in, editorial writers and other media observers quickly announced their verdict—a stunning defeat for the LDP, a rebuke of Tanaka-style political methods, the beginning of the end for the conservatives, a possible legislative halt in the House of Councillors—in effect, a near miss for the opposition. The reason for the initial surprised reaction was the excessive media optimism for the LDP and pessimism for the opposition's ability to work together effectively in the cooperation districts. The news media had stressed controversial and attention-getting developments—corruption, infla-

---

[22] This theory was behind the LDP's decision to extend voting time by one hour.

[23] See Appendix, Table A-4, for figures on upper house elections since 1947.

Table 3-2

SEATS WON, VOTE AND PERCENTAGE OF THE VOTE,
BY PARTY, HOUSE OF COUNCILLORS ELECTION, 1974

Party	National Constituency			Local Constituencies		
	Seats won	Vote	Percentage of total vote	Seats won	Vote	Percentage of total vote
LDP	19	23,332,773	44.3	43	21,132,372	39.5
JSP	10	7,990,456	15.2	18	13,907,864	26.0
KMT	9	6,360,419	12.1	5	6,732,937	12.6
JCP	8	4,931,649	9.4	5	6,428,919	12.0
DSP	4	3,114,895	5.9	1	2,353,397	4.4
Other	4	6,894,544	13.1	4	2,941,911	5.5
Total	54	52,624,736	100.0	76	53,497,400	100.0

Source: Central Election Management Committee.

tion, the vast sums being spent in the campaign, Tanaka's helicopter forays into local constituencies in the campaign's hectic final days. Whether and how these specific issues and events shaped the outcome is uncertain, but it seems clear that unrealistic expectations caused media commentators—and many party officials as well—to swing too far away from their previous views in their postelection analyses. These dim post-mortems of the conservative performance to the contrary, the LDP "defeat" was not sweeping. Without doubt Tanaka and the LDP lost the public relations battle, but the party's actual performance was mixed.

To assess the performance of the LDP and the other parties in the 1974 election and to place the results of this one election in a longer-term context, some objective standards are needed. To make the discussion here as systematic as possible, vote totals and percentages and number of seats are the data employed in evaluating aggregate results and party performance. Where it is useful to do so, these figures are correlated with past upper house election data, by national and local constituency, district type (number of seats), and candidate characteristics (such as sex, occupation, age, previous experience in the House of Councillors). Finally, data are measured against election district type, classified according to degree of "urbanization." Watanuki has found urbanization to be the most significant of all major variables influencing Japanese voting behavior and hence electoral performance.[24] The analysis here employs a classificatory scheme using the urbanization variable, which has been adapted from that used with good results by the *Sankei Shimbun* in its election coverage. Under this system, districts are grouped into five categories (labelled A, B, C, D, E) according to their percentage of primary industry and of persons employed in primary industry.[25]

The Polls. In the 1971 upper house election practically every newspaper underestimated the strength of the JSP and overestimated that of the LDP. Of all the newspapers the *Asahi* was the only one to call the outcome correctly (allowing for statistical error). As shown in Table 3-3, the polls were again wide of the mark in 1974—by an even greater margin—and again by underestimation of JSP and overestimation of LDP (and this time also of KMT) performance. Except for JCP gains, they predicted a confirmation of the status quo for all. As in 1971 the *Asahi* predictions were the most reliable, particularly their estimate of vote percentages (see Table 3-4), which the paper calculated to within 1 percent for all but two of the parties.[26] Of all preelection prognoses those of the *Asahi* also came closest in picking the number of seats each party would receive. Allowing for statistical error, the *Asahi* forecast missed by only three seats. In general, national-constituency projections were more accurate than those for the local constituencies. But even for the national constituency, the forecasts (except that of the *Asahi*) failed to anticipate the size of the independent vote or the drop in Sōhyō support for the JSP. In general, projections were more accurate for "talent" and labor candidates than for ex-bureaucrats and representatives of religious organizations. At

[24] Joji Watanuki, "Japanese Politics in Flux," in James William Morley, ed., *Prologue to the Future* (Lexington, Mass.: D. C. Heath and Company, 1974), pp. 71, 76.

[25] See *Sankei Shimbun*, 10 July 1974. Figures are based on 1970 census data and represent the combination of two indices—the proportion of primary industry to total industry in a given district and the percentage of the total district population employed in the primary sector. *"A"* or *metropolitan* districts (under 10 percent) are: Tokyo, Kanagawa, Aichi, Kyoto, and Osaka; *"B"* or *urban* (10 to 20 percent): Saitama, Shizuoka, Hyogo, Nara, Hiroshima, Fukuoka; *"C"* or *semi-urban* (20 to 30 percent): Hokkaido, Tochigi, Gumma, Chiba, Yamanashi, Toyama, Ishikawa, Fukui, Gifu, Mie, Shiga, Wakayama, Okayama, Yamaguchi, Kagawa, Ehime, Nagasaki; *"D"* or *semi-rural* (30 to 40 percent): Yamagata, Fukushima, Ibaragi, Niigata, Nagano, Tottori, Shimane, Tokushima, Kochi, Saga, Kumamoto, Oita, Miyazaki, and Miyagi; and *"E"* or *rural* (40 percent plus): Aomori, Iwate, Akita, and Kagoshima. (Okinawa excluded.) Passin (pp. 39-41) uses a somewhat different classification, but the two systems show similar trends. Passin's scheme of measuring the degree of urbanization is based on 1970 census data on population density and statistics on internal migration from 1965 to 1970.

[26] *Asahi Shimbun*, 26 June 1974; compare *Mainichi Shimbun*, 3 July 1974.

Table 3-3

NEWSPAPER PREDICTIONS OF NUMBER OF WINNING CANDIDATES, BY PARTY, AND ACTUAL RESULTS, HOUSE OF COUNCILLORS ELECTION, 1974[a]

	Asahi	Nihon Keizai	Mainichi	Yomiuri	Sankei	Actual
National constituency						
LDP	23 (19–27)	22 (21–24)	21 (20–24)	24 (21–27)	23 (21–25)	19
JSP	8 (5–11)	9 (8–10)	9 (7–11)	10 (7–12)	8 (8–10)	10
KMT	9 (8–9)	9	9	8 (8–9)	9	9
DSP	3 (2–4)	3 (3–4)	4 (3–4)	3 (2–4)	3 (3–4)	4
JCP	7 (6–8)	7 (7–8)	7 (7–8)	6 (5–8)	8 (7–8)	8
Other	4 (3–5)	4 (4–5)	4 (3–4)	3 (2–4)	3 (3–4)	4
Local constituencies						
LDP	47 (43–51)	49 (47–52)	51 (49–52)	49 (46–52)	50 (49–53)	43
JSP	17 (14–20)	15 (12–19)	14 (13–16)	16 (12–19)	16 (14–16)	18
KMT	6 (4–8)	5 (3–5)	3 (2–4)	3 (2–5)	2 (1–4)	5
DSP	1 (0–2)	1 (0–2)	1 (1–2)	1 (0–2)	1 (0–2)	1
JCP	7 (6–8)	4 (2–5)	4 (4–5)	4 (3–5)	4 (3–4)	5
Other	2 (0–3)	2 (1–4)	3 (2–4)	3 (1–5)	3 (2–3)	4
All constituencies						
LDP	70 (65–75)	71 (68–76)	72 (69–76)	73 (67–79)	73 (70–78)	62
JSP	25 (21–29)	24 (20–29)	23 (20–27)	26 (19–31)	24 (22–26)	28
KMT	15 (13–17)	14 (13–14)	12 (11–13)	11 (10–14)	11 (10–13)	14
DSP	4 (2–6)	4 (3–6)	5 (4–6)	4 (2–6)	4 (3–6)	5
JCP	10 (8–12)	11 (9–13)	11 (9–13)	10 (8–13)	12 (10–12)	13
Other	6 (3–7)	6 (5–9)	7 (5–8)	6 (3–9)	6 (5–7)	8

a Figures in parentheses indicate each newspaper's estimate of the range of possible winning candidates, allowing for statistical error.

Sources: *Asahi Shimbun*, 25 June 1974; *Nihon Keizai Shimbun*, 4 July 1974; *Mainichi Shimbun*, 3 July 1974; *Yomiuri Shimbun*, 1 July 1974; *Sankei Shimbun*, 5 July 1974.

Table 3-4

NEWSPAPER PREDICTIONS OF PARTY VOTE AND ACTUAL
RESULTS, HOUSE OF COUNCILLORS ELECTION, 1974

(in percents)

Party	National Constituency			Local Constituencies		
	Asahi	*Mainichi*	Actual	*Asahi*	*Mainichi*	Actual
LDP	44.6	46.4	44.3	39.0	39.4	39.5
JSP	13.5	15.2	15.2	24.8	24.7	26.0
KMT	12.3	14.3	12.1	13.6	13.7	12.6
DSP	5.6	5.6	5.9	4.7	3.8	4.4
JCP	9.4	8.5	9.4	12.4	12.5	12.0
Other	14.6	10.0	13.1	5.5	5.9	5.5

Sources: *Asahi Shimbun*, 25 June 1974; *Mainichi Shimbun*, 3 July 1974.

least eight LDP losers were picked to win by two or more major newspaper surveys. And extreme instances of inaccuracy abound: one *Yomiuri* writer picked LDP candidate Tanaka Tadao to finish sixth, while in fact he wound up fifty-seventh!

Profile of Winning Candidates. As compared with previous upper house elections, more winning candidates were running for the first time in the 1974 contest. New candidates performed better (71 of 130 total winners were new, or 54.6 percent) than in any House of Councillors election since 1953. New candidates did well in both the national and local constituencies: nationally, 28 of 54 winners were new (51.85 percent); locally, 43 of 76 (76.3 percent). There were eighteen more new winners in the local constituencies than in 1971 and more than in any election since 1956. By contrast, as illustrated in Figure 3-2, office holders in the local constituencies fared badly: only 67 percent won as against the usual 80 percent.

Among all the political parties in 1974 the LDP ran the fewest new candidates (nineteen of thirty-five in the national constituency, twenty-six of sixty in the local constituencies), but its new candidates performed better (eleven winning nationally, twenty-one locally) than its incumbents. Of the top ten LDP national-constituency winners, seven were new and three were incumbents (in 1971 this had been five and five). Seventeen LDP incumbents lost in 1974, six nationally and eleven locally.

Figure 3-2

PERCENTAGE OF CANDIDATES WINNING,
NEW AND INCUMBENT, LOCAL CONSTITUENCIES,
HOUSE OF COUNCILLORS ELECTIONS, 1959–1974

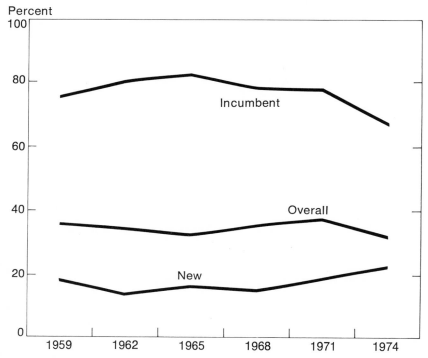

Source: Based on statistics from the Ministry of Home Affairs.

Age. It seemed in some ways that the younger generation was challenging the old in the 1974 election. But it is uncertain from the data whether youth constituted an advantage, all other factors held constant, except perhaps in the national constituency. The average national-constituency winner in 1974 was slightly younger than the average national-constituency candidate (winners, fifty-three; overall national, fifty-four). But in the local constituencies, the average winner was six years older than the average candidate (winners, fifty-six; overall local, fifty).

Women. Of the women standing for election in the prefectural constituencies, three won—two members of the JCP in Hyogo and Hokkaido, and one the wife of a former LDP prefectural governor in

Table 3-5

WOMEN CANDIDATES AND WINNERS, HOUSE OF COUNCILLORS ELECTIONS, 1947–1974

Election	National Constituency		Local Constituencies		All Constituencies	
	Nominated	Elected	Nominated	Elected	Nominated	Elected
1947	13	8	6	2	19	10
1950	15	3	9	2	24	5
1953	17	5	11	4	28	9
1956	10	3	7	2	17	5
1959	10	5	8	3	18	8
1962	9	6	6	2	15	8
1965	8	7	5	2	13	9
1968	8	4	3	1	11	5
1971	9	5	6	3	15	8
1974	9	5	9	3	18	8

Sources: 1947 to 1971 figures are from the Ministry of Home Affairs; 1974 data are from the Central Election Management Committee.

Ibaragi who ran as a "recommended" LDP candidate without official party endorsement. In the national constituency there were also nine women running, of whom five won—the eighty-one-year-old independent, Ichikawa Fusae; two LDP "talents," Santō Akiko and Yamaguchi Yoshiko; a JSP representative of the Japan Teachers Union, Kasuya Teruko; and one Communist, Yamanaka Ikuko. Of eighteen women candidates, these eight were successful. These figures were similar to those for past upper house elections, as is illustrated in Table 3-5.

Preelection surveys indicated that in the 1974 national-constituency election about 70 percent of those who supported Ichikawa, Santō, and Yamanaka were women, as were over 80 percent of those who supported Yamaguchi. Kasuya had roughly balanced support from men and women.[27] In the local constituencies the JCP nominated more women than any other party. Its four women ran in urban multimember districts with some success: one was the top winner in Hokkaido and another was the third winner in Hyogo.

[27] *Mainichi Shimbun*, 12 July 1974.

Women outvoted men in the 1974 election in twenty-six of the forty-seven districts, including half the two-member constituencies. Further, a slightly greater percentage of the eligible women voted than men (73.63 to 72.73 percent), continuing a trend since 1968 (see Appendix, Figure A-2). More women voted in the multimember districts (except Aichi and Hokkaido) and, since conservatives did poorly in these areas, one may infer that many women voted "progressive," and most likely for the JCP. In the national constituency, too, with the JSP voting rate down 6 percent and the independents' up 8 percent, it is probable that many women cast ballots for the Communist and Kōmeitō candidates.[28]

Organizational Support Structures. 1974 election results revealed only minor shifts in longer-term patterns of performance among political support structures. Media exaggerations notwithstanding, the traditional sectors were still generating votes. The fluctuations that did exist seem to have been most directly related to changes in the composition and particularly in the socioeconomic structure of the Japanese electorate. The economic and social transformation of Japan was mirrored in the election results.

Generalizations about performance in the national constituency are complicated by the fact that many candidates in 1974 received support from several organizations. Moreover, there were important differences among the various organizations in the strength of their support and variations in the strength of support from any one organization over time. Still, some general propositions can be offered on the support structure for this election—how it differed from the structure of earlier support and how current trends may shape future elections. First, as in the past, victory in Japan's unique national-constituency arena depended on whether a candidate was well known or had an extensive (ideally national) organizational support structure. Second, with a few exceptions, it appears that a single organization is no longer a sufficient vehicle for success in the national constituency. The highest-ranked candidates in 1974 had multiple tributaries of support. Even "talent," in and of itself, was no guarantee of success, as several losing and borderline *tarento* candidates discovered. Top "talent" finishers also had several organizations behind them. Third, it seems that even though candidates backed by primary-sector organizations fared poorly in the national constituency, compared to the way they performed in 1971, they showed considerable strength in the local contests. Fourth, business support appeared more frail

---

28 Ibid.

than the backing of other organizations. The much-vaunted company loyalty of the Japanese did not extend to voting for a particular candidate simply because that candidate was supported by his employer. Nor did it seem to matter to the voters that a candidate had the endorsement of the manufacturer of a popular brand of cosmetics, toothpaste, or automobile. Finally, the election suggested that it will be increasingly difficult for future national-constituency candidates to win unless they can appeal to the urban population. Metropolitan and urban (A-, B-type) areas, after all, include nearly half the total national-constituency votes. In the 1974 election, "talent," corporation-backed LDP, and JCP and KMT candidates had the greatest appeal in these A- and B-type areas. By contrast, ex-bureaucrats and organizational representatives attracted a predominantly semi-urban, semi-rural, or rural (C-, D-, E-type) vote.

Labor. The trend in upper house elections is toward fewer labor-union-backed candidates, even though those supported by labor nearly always win in the national constituency. In the 1965 House of Councillors election, ten of fourteen Sōhyō-backed JSP national candidates won; in 1968, eight of eleven; and in 1971, eight of nine. Dōmei has had only slightly less success: two of four in 1965 and all four in 1968 and 1971.

But labor-union-supported candidates have attracted fewer and fewer votes in recent upper house elections. Leftist-oriented candidates backed by Nikkyōso (Japan Teachers Union) secured 400,000 fewer votes in 1971 than they had six years before, and Jichirō (All Japan Prefectural and Municipal Workers Union) representatives, 200,000 fewer. Furthermore, the JCP made inroads into certain Sōhyō unions, particularly Nikkyōso and Jichirō. The JCP urged union members to reject designated JSP candidates, using the slogan "Freedom of Party Support" (*seitō shiji no jiyū*), an appealing theme for the 1974 election, particularly for younger workers. The rebuttal in the union newspaper by anxious Sōhyō officials had a less ambiguous headline: "Freedom not to vote JCP." Weakened JSP support among rank-and-file members of the so-called "Three Sōhyō Houses" (Jichirō, Nikkyōso, and Dōrō) had splintered some local organizations. Twenty-six local Nikkyōso chapters, for instance, many of them in urban prefectures, had taken on the freedom-of-party-support doctrine as their guiding principle.[29] Surveys also indicated less political consciousness among Dōmei workers than before and as a result the number of labor union members uncommitted to the DSP had risen,

---

[29] *Asahi Shimbun*, 4 July 1974.

especially in the textile and ship workers' unions.[30] At the Maritime Workers Union convention in late 1973 the issue of freedom of party support was central, although the union eventually decided to back the DSP candidate. In the end, three-fourths of the JSP and over a third of the DSP candidates had had some labor union experience.

Despite all this, labor-backed candidates won convincingly in 1974. All thirteen national-constituency candidates representing labor (eight JCP, four DSP, one independent) won, with fairly high rankings. In vote totals, these candidates received 9 million votes, or 17 percent of all national-constituency votes cast. While this was a far cry from the 1956 election when forty-six labor and labor-supported candidates had won, the 1974 results suggest a bottoming out of the long-term decline in labor candidate performance.

Religious organizations. In the 1971 election there were five candidates representing religious organizations, of whom two were successful. Nine other candidates (including five more winners) had at least some backing from religious groups. Religious groups, with the exception of the KMT's Sōka Gakkai, support the LDP. Fourteen national-constituency LDP candidates were wholly or partially supported by religious organizations for the 1974 election, exactly the same number as in 1971. On the strength of its showing in 1971, Seichō no Ie, an ultraconservative militant sect that favored passage of the controversial Yasukuni Shrine bill,[31] supported two candidates in 1974—the first time the sect had supported two. Risshō Kōseikai provided the main base of support for candidate Nagano Chinyū. Other religious organizations—PL Kyōdan, Tenrikyō, Reiyūkai— backed nine other LDP candidates whose principal support came from other groups. One of these candidates, popular ex-bureaucrat Hato-yama Iichirō, was endorsed by religious groups on both sides of the Yasukuni Shrine issue.

Preelection surveys indicated that religious candidates were supported mainly by women, voters in their forties or older, those engaged in light manufacturing, and persons living in farming and

---

[30] According to one source, only 17 percent of the Maritime Workers Union members supported the DSP in 1974. The same percentage supported the LDP (Fuji Telecasting Company, *Documents for the 10th Upper House Election,* 7 July 1974). See also *Mainichi Shimbun,* 26 June 1974.

[31] The Yasukuni Shrine is a memorial to Japan's war dead, located in Tokyo. The LDP introduced legislation in 1973 which would have provided subsidies to the shrine. Critics objected on the grounds that such support was constitutionally forbidden. Articles 20 and 89 of the Japanese constitution bar the government from engaging in religious activities and from using public money to subsidize such activities.

Figure 3-3

DISTRIBUTION OF TOTAL NATIONAL CONSTITUENCY VOTE,
BY DEGREE OF URBANIZATION,
HOUSE OF COUNCILLORS ELECTION, 1974

(in percents)

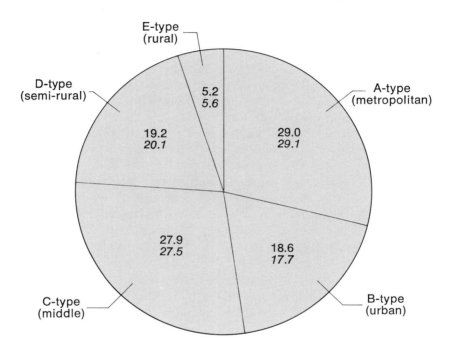

Note: Top figures are for 1974; lower figures are for the 1971 upper house election.

Source: Calculated from statistics of the Ministry of Home Affairs and the Central Election Management Committee.

fishing areas.[32] Election results tended to confirm the belief that candidates whose main support base was a religious group would perform marginally better outside the metropolitan (A-type) districts than the LDP as a whole did nationally (see Figure 3-3). Otherwise, in the metropolitan, urban, and semi-urban (A-, B-, and C-type) districts they were stronger than LDP bureaucrats and other orga-

[32] For example, an *Asahi Shimbun* poll, published on 29 June 1974, estimated that Risshō Kōseikai candidate Hasegawa Jin's potential constituency was 70-80 percent women.

101

nizational representatives but weaker than the *tarento* and "enterprise" candidates.

The high voting rate seems to have left behind those LDP candidates supported solely by religious groups. Both Seichō no Ie candidates lost, by under 15,000 votes each, and both Risshō Kōseikai aspirants were defeated as well. Had each organization run just one candidate, the LDP would have had two more seats in the new House of Councillors and these groups would have had legislative spokesmen.

Other interest groups. The number of winners representing special interest groups dropped steadily from twenty in 1959 to twelve in 1969 and to eight in 1971. Of eleven candidates of this type in the 1974 election, only five won, and the relative ranking of organizational representatives by votes declined.

In general, the segments of Japanese society that favor religious-type candidates also support special-interest organizational representatives.[33] A combination of three factors—the high voting rate, changes in the Japanese electorate, and more diffuse foundations of public support—made interest group candidates do more poorly in 1974 than in 1971, both in votes received and in relative ranking. In the preceding election five of eight such candidates won—those representing the Bereaved Families Association, nurses, dentists, wartime pensioners, and the Kajima Construction Company. Those running with the support of the pharmacists, doctors, midwives, and the unofficial backing of members of the Self-Defense Agency lost. In 1974, five of eleven survived the national-constituency tests, with the bereaved families, wartime pensioners, Kajima Construction, and doctors on the winning side. Candidates representing dentists, midwives, school teachers, the Milk Producers Association, and the Chamber of Commerce lost. Further, special interest candidates ranked lower overall in 1974 than in 1971, although the relative standing of the winners in both elections was about the same. Ōtani Hiroshi and Okada Katsunosuke, LDP winners who represented, respectively, the Bereaved Families Association and the wartime pensioners, did slightly better than expected, though the total votes cast for these groups' candidates declined from their 1971 levels, perhaps indicating their diminishing appeal to the postwar generation.

Ex-bureaucrats. The thirty bureaucratic candidates (twenty-nine LDP, one DSP) achieved about the same results as in the last election, though eight LDP candidates of this type lost locally and one na-

---

[33] *Asahi Shimbun*, 29 June 1974.

tionally.[34] Of the eight LDP prefectural losses, all but one occurred in two-member or multimember districts. Of winning LDP ex-bureaucrats running in the national constituency, the top five were from two ministries—Construction, and Agriculture and Forestry. It was thought that the recession in the building industry and the government's unpopular agricultural policy might hurt these candidates. Instead, their relatively high rankings demonstrated once again that a bureaucratic background is a strong if not necessarily winning support base for the national constituency. Only one LDP bureaucratic candidate failed in the national contest (Okabe Tamotsu). Interestingly, most of the "bureaucratic" vote was in C-, D-, and E-type districts or was distributed evenly in all five varieties of district, a fact that underlines the appeal of this type of candidate to more traditional sectors of the population. At the same time those candidates who received high support from their home prefectures tended to do better than those without.[35] The LDP was somewhat less dependent than in past elections upon the "bureaucratic" vote in the national constituency. Ex-bureaucrat LDP candidates received 30 percent of all the party's national-constituency votes, as against 40 percent in 1971.

Business. The LDP endorsed many candidates (twenty of ninety-five) with business experience or corporate backing. For its public image, the party's heavy reliance upon "enterprise" candidates in the national campaign was disastrous. These candidates succeeded only when they had other sources of support (like bureaucrat Satō Shinji) or were well known (like "talent" candidate Yamaguchi). The two LDP candidates from big business (*zaikai*) backgrounds, Itoyama Eitarō and Morishita Tai, also had other support. Itoyama had written a best-selling book. Morishita, who owned a large pharmaceutical company, was also backed by Suntory, associations of pharmaceutical wholesalers, and martial arts societies. "Pure" enterprise candidates

---

[34] The proportion of ex-bureaucrats among all LDP candidates in 1974 was about the same as it had been in previous upper house elections and roughly the same as the party's bureaucratic representation in the House of Councillors, where 50 of the 135 LDP members had had bureaucratic experience. Of the 29 LDP bureaucratic candidates (see Table 3-1) six were from the Ministry of Construction, five each from the Police Agency or former Home Ministry and the Ministry of Agriculture and Forestry, four from the Ministry of Finance, three from the Ministry of Posts and Telecommunications, and one each from the following ministries and agencies: Justice, Labor, Transportation, Welfare, Self-Defense, and National Railways. Seven had climbed to the pinnacle of Japanese officialdom—the vice-ministerships—and a majority of the rest were one step behind, having served as bureau chiefs. Nine ran in the national constituency, where very few candidates with bureaucratic backgrounds have ever lost.

[35] Examples of strong showings in home districts by ex-bureaucrats are Marumo Shigesada in Gumma and Sakomizu Hisatsune in Kagoshima.

were relatively weak, with uneven support, one example being Saka Ken, the unknown running with Mitsubishi backing. Saka—and several top Mitsubishi executives—campaigned harder but finished lower than any other major LDP national candidate.[36] Saka did receive some 70–80 percent of the vote he was expected to gain in Mitsubishi areas, but this was not enough. Similarly, the well-known former women's volleyball coach Daimatsu Hirobumi garnered little support from his sponsors, Idemitsu and Toshiba Electric, leaving him with less than a third of his winning 1968 total. Tamaki Tadao failed to generate much enthusiasm at Kawasaki Steel, and Nagano Chinyū did only slightly better with New Japan Steel. Santō Akiko, a popular actress, had much better luck with Hitachi, gaining over three times her projected vote in Hitachi districts.[37] Satō Shinji, the former prime minister's second son, received fairly good support from the company that manufactures Mazda automobiles. Yamaguchi, another who was both an "enterprise" and a "talent" candidate, did far worse than expected—her victory was not confirmed until long past midnight on election night.

A business background, however, was a definite asset in the local races. There were more business-related LDP winners this time than in 1971 and of twenty business candidates, fourteen were elected.

Agriculture. In the national constituency, with over 5 million rural households, the agricultural sector has virtually guaranteed victory for three to four LDP candidates in past elections. Moreover, rural winners have attained high rankings: agricultural "seats" in the national constituency since 1953 have ranked as high as third, seventh, eighth, and eleventh. In the local constituencies, too, the influence of rural notables has been telling: the most powerful local figure has commonly headed the local farmers' association (nōkyō).

Now there are far fewer nōkyō units than there were—down to slightly over 5,000 from 12,000 a decade ago. In addition, the local agricultural organization has been weakened by inroads by the labor unions. Forty percent of the local nōkyō organizations have been unionized. Rural support for the JCP has also risen, and there is a slightly enlarged rural uncommitted or independent "floating vote" (up three percentage points since 1971).[38] The support of the membership of a local nōkyō for a designated candidate is no longer automatic. Low rice prices have also aroused anti-LDP sentiment in rural districts. In the 1971 election some LDP campaign posters in

---

[36] Saka's campaign is described in detail in the Curtis essay, pp. 66-69.
[37] *Yomiuri Shimbun,* 10 July 1974.
[38] *Asahi Shimbun,* 29 May 1974.

rural areas had the words "LDP-endorsed" printed in black on a dark blue background—safely illegible from a distance. In 1974 rural support for the LDP again seemed tenuous. Many of the rural citizenry believed that the LDP had deserted their interests by courting "talent" and "enterprise" candidates for the national campaign.

In 1974 no national candidate ran solely with *nōkyō* support, inasmuch as the rural vote by itself was insufficient for election. The leading national agricultural organization (Zenryōren) could promise only 350,000 votes to a prospective candidate—far beneath the projected 550,000-vote winning threshold. Two men considered running under the LDP banner but backed out, leaving just two LDP national-constituency candidates with partial agricultural support—Kamei Zenshō and Kobayashi Kuniji. In the local constituencies, however, there were ten *nōkyō*-related candidates, including five in the pivotal two-member districts. While Kamei was buried in the election, Kobayashi (a former bureaucrat with strong nonrural backing) won handily, as did all but one of the *nōkyō* local candidates. The one who failed (Kawaguchi Yōichi in Hokkaido) lost because of an LDP tactical mistake, not because of *nōkyō* weakness. All *nōkyō* candidates won in the two-member districts, and Sonoda Hiroyuki scored a conspicuous win in Kumamoto, a prefecture with 20,000 fewer rural households than in 1968. Also notable was Kujime Kentarō's successful race for the one seat in Tokushima. As discussed elsewhere in this volume, the Kujime-Gotōda clash in Tokushima was seized upon by the press as a litmus test of public feelings about corruption and Tanaka's high-handed electioneering. Kujime had failed to win the LDP endorsement and had run as an independent. But, though his opponent was Tanaka's hand-picked candidate, Kujime had the support of most of the prefecture's 180,000 people engaged in agriculture and fishing. It is therefore possible to view Kujime's triumph in Tokushima as a demonstration of the continuing, if somewhat lessened, ability of *nōkyō* to deliver the rural vote.[39]

Party Performance

Data relating to the urbanization variable are of particular significance in assessing the performance of the various parties and the longer-range implications of the election. As a basis for analysis, Figures 3-3 and 3-4 portray, first, the configuration of the total 1974 national-constituency vote, by district type, using the urbanization variable

---

[39] Curtis, pp. 77-79.

Figure 3-4

DISTRIBUTION OF NATIONAL-CONSTITUENCY VOTE BY PARTY AND DISTRICT TYPE
(DEGREE OF URBANIZATION), HOUSE OF COUNCILLORS ELECTION, 1974

(in percents)

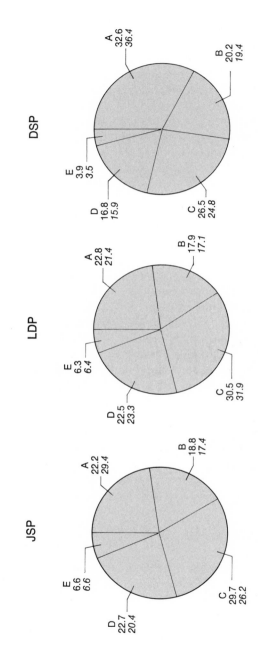

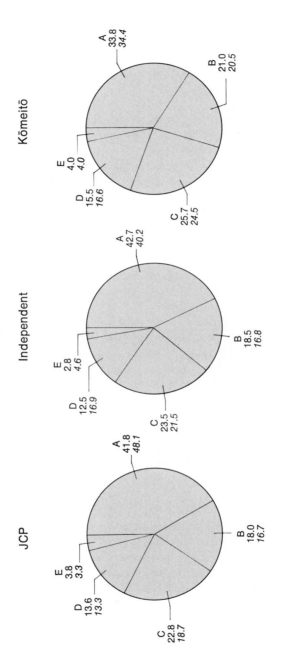

JCP

Independent

Kōmeitō

A 41.8 48.1

A 42.7 40.2

A 33.8 34.4

B 18.0 16.7

B 18.5 16.8

B 21.0 20.5

C 22.8 18.7

C 23.5 21.5

C 25.7 24.5

D 13.6 13.3

D 12.5 16.9

D 15.5 16.6

E 3.8 3.3

E 2.8 4.6

E 4.0 4.0

Note: Top figures are for 1974; lower figures are for the 1971 upper house election.
Source: Calculated from statistics of the Ministry of Home Affairs and the Central Election Management Committee.

(A-E district classification); and second, the distribution of the party and independent vote, based on the same system. As these diagrams suggest, while the distribution of the total 1974 national-constituency vote was virtually the same as the distribution of the vote in 1971, the configuration of each party's vote shifted, in some cases rather dramatically.

Independents. One of the features of the 1974 election was the record independent vote in the national constituency—6.7 million votes,[40] or 13.1 percent of the total. Two candidates, Ichikawa Fusae and Aoshima Yukio, who finished second and third, took roughly half these votes. The 1974 independent vote was three times the 1971 independent vote. It exceeded 10 percent for the first time since the politicization of the House of Councillors in 1962.[41] As the diagrams in Figure 3-4 suggest, the appeal of the independent candidates was concentrated in the metropolitan and urban (A- and B-type) districts, which have a high proportion of the floating vote, more than it was in the 1971 election. Independents took a surprising 18.6 percent of the vote in A- and B-type districts, as compared with 7.3 percent in 1971. In these districts the independents were second to the LDP, and in Tokyo independents were less than three percentage points behind the LDP. But the 1974 independent vote increase was nation-wide, extending to the less urbanized areas with a low floating vote as well. Independent Aoshima, for example, won 4.1 percent of the total national-constituency vote in conservative Tokushima prefecture.

While the independent vote increase may reflect an anti-party reaction, one should note that 45 percent of the independent vote went to the independent "talent" candidates and that it was not so much the LDP as the "progressive" parties, especially the KMT and the JSP, that were hurt by the independents in the national constituency.

LDP: Crisis of Expectations. The LDP won nine fewer local and four fewer national seats than predicted in most forecasts. But these "losses" must be measured carefully against inflated preelection hopes for the LDP in some districts that were simply too close to call. The setbacks the LDP did encounter resulted from ill-advised tactics (such as running too many candidates in Hokkaido) and the high voting rate.

Although the number of eligible voters rose by nearly one-third over the decade from 1964 to 1974, LDP support, measured by votes

---

[40] Excluding "bubble" candidates, this figure is 6.3 million.
[41] See Passin, pp. 13-14 and 27-29.

received, did not change much. One newspaper, the *Asahi*, estimated that (assuming an LDP support rate of 30.5 percent and an electorate of 75.7 million) there were 23.1 million potential LDP voters. Using the past three elections as a guide, *Asahi* analysts further reasoned that about 80 percent of the LDP "supporters" would vote along party lines, producing 18.5 million LDP votes.[42] When the final count was in, however, the LDP had for the first time matched its support rate (101 percent) and had received 23.3 million votes—far beyond its vote totals in the three previous elections.

A close analysis of the figures, moreover, reveals that the LDP obtained a sizable portion of the 14 percent increase in the overall national-constituency vote. One election post-mortem estimated that the LDP had garnered 53 percent of this increase[43]—although it is hard to judge to what extent, if at all, this worked to the LDP's advantage.

Although the LDP's percentage of the national-constituency vote was virtually unchanged from 1971, its share of the metropolitan or A-type district vote was somewhat higher. In the metropolitan areas the LDP national candidates outpolled their local-constituency LDP counterparts by nearly 1.4 million votes. Moreover, the proportion of the party's national-constituency vote that was concentrated in the A-type districts was over 4 percent larger than the corresponding proportion of its local-constituency vote. The LDP more than held its own against the sharp rise in the 1974 independent vote.

The LDP also was able to raise its share of the rural or D- and E-type district vote over 1971. The LDP, of course, has depended most heavily on rural support, and the 1974 election showed a continuation of this dependence. In the rural and semi-rural districts the LDP vote, which was 5.6 million in 1968 and 5.3 million in 1971, climbed to 6.7 million in 1974. These districts have awarded the LDP seventeen, sixteen, and seventeen seats in the past three elections, and an increasing share of the vote: 51.2, 51.4, and 52.3 percent. By any measure the rural areas remain the stronghold of the conservatives.

One reason why the LDP was able to perform creditably in the national constituency in 1974 was that each of the party's main candidate types—"talents," ex-bureaucrats, and organizational repre-

[42] *Asahi Shimbun*, 26 June 1974.

[43] *Asahi Jyānaru*, 19 July 1974, p. 6. As of February 1976 the distribution of upper house seats among the parties was LDP, 129; JSP, 62; KMT, 24; JCP, 20; DSP, 10; Niin Club, 5; Ind., 2; and no vacancies.

sentatives—tends to appeal to different voters. This is illustrated by the diagrams in Figure 3-5.

As these diagrams suggest, the improved 1974 LDP performance in the A-type or metropolitan districts was probably due to the appeal of the LDP "talent" candidates. Nearly 32 percent of the LDP's metropolitan vote was taken by the "talents." And one explanation for the continued LDP domination of the rural and semi-rural districts is the drawing power of ex-bureaucrat candidates in these areas. Nearly half of all LDP votes in the national constituency and over one-fourth of all votes cast in the rural districts went to the party's nine former bureaucrats. The LDP's organizational candidates had an urban-rural vote distribution pattern quite similar to that of the party as a whole (see Figure 3-4).

In the local prefectural constituencies in 1974, the LDP would have had to take over half the fourteen-percentage-point increase over the 1971 vote for this increase to have helped the party. But the LDP received less than one-third of the increase. Among all prefectural constituencies only Fukui (one-member) and Kumamoto (two-member) gave the LDP over 60 percent of the vote, compared with ten such districts in 1968 and six in 1971.

Several indicators of performance—percentage of the vote, number of seats won, and vote totals—are given in Table 3-6 for

Table 3-6

LDP PERCENTAGE OF VOTE, VOTE TOTALS, AND SEATS WON, IN ONE-, TWO-, AND MULTIMEMBER DISTRICTS, HOUSE OF COUNCILLORS ELECTIONS, 1962–1974[a]

	One-Member			Two-Member			Multimember		
	Percent of vote	Vote total	No. of seats	Percent of vote	Vote total	No. of seats	Percent of vote	Vote total	No. of seats
1962	52.80	6.2	22	48.41	6.2	16	40.00	4.7	9
1965	49.96	5.9	21	49.93	6.6	17	32.99	4.2	8
1968	51.70	6.6	20	51.37	7.8	21	32.62	5.0	7
1971	47.56	5.8	16	49.32	7.2	16	33.93	4.7	9
1974	49.55	7.5	24	43.31	8.6	14	27.17	5.0	5

[a] Vote totals in millions; figures exclude conservative-related independents.
Sources: 1962–1971 election figures are based on statistics from the House of Councillors Administrative Affairs Bureau and the Ministry of Home Affairs; 1974 data are from the Central Election Management Committee.

Figure 3-5

DISTRIBUTION OF LDP NATIONAL-CONSTITUENCY VOTE BY CANDIDATE TYPE, HOUSE OF COUNCILLORS ELECTION, 1974

(in percents)

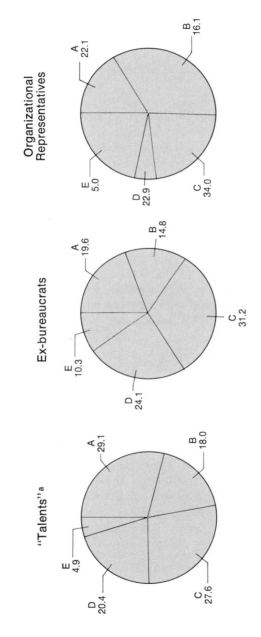

"Talents"[a]

Ex-bureaucrats

Organizational Representatives

[a] If Miyata Teru's huge and evenly distributed vote is excluded, nearly 35 percent of the LDP "talent" vote was concentrated in the A-type districts.

Source: Derived from vote totals provided by the Central Election Management Committee and published in the *Asahi Shimbun*, 9 July 1974.

local-constituency contests in the past five upper house elections. The LDP swept all but two of the one-member districts in 1974, winning more seats, votes, and a higher percentage of the vote than in 1971. Only two one-member-district races (Shimane and Yamanashi) were even close. But except for total votes and the record of these one-member prefectural districts, however, all indicators point to an LDP decline.

The impression of LDP decline in the two-member districts is moderated only slightly if the percentages listed in Table 3-6 are adjusted to include votes for winning conservative independent candidates who later joined the LDP. Presumably the votes cast in these elections for these candidates were potentially LDP votes; adding these votes to the total might therefore portray conservative strength and LDP potential with greater precision. Adding these votes results in the following figures: [44]

	1968	1971	1974
One-member districts	54.47	48.85	50.84
Two-member districts	53.82	49.32	46.33

Another perspective may be reached by excluding entirely those districts in which conservative-related candidates stood for election, as follows:

	1968	1971	1974
One-member districts	55.26	52.36	49.86
Two-member districts	53.23	49.47	45.55

All the manipulations of the figures show a gradual decline in LDP and conservative support.[45] Whether lower voting percentages will adversely affect the party in the future is less certain. In only five two-member districts has the LDP vote declined more than five percentage points from 1962 to 1974. However, these five districts are in any case not party strongholds. In these districts the LDP captured both seats on just three occasions (Gumma, 1968; Shizuoka, 1962 and 1968). Further, even though the LDP has lost ground in the two-member districts since 1962,[46] when one compares 1974 with 1971,

---

[44] The 1974 figures include votes for conservative independents recommended but not endorsed by the LDP in Tochigi and Ibaragi (two-member districts) and for conservative Kujime Kentarō in Tokushima (one-member district).

[45] A gradual LDP decline since 1962 is also apparent if one calculates LDP seats won as a percentage of total seats won: 1962—54.3, 1965—55.9, 1968—54.7, 1971—49.6, and 1974—47.7.

[46] The LDP received 2.4 million of a 7.1-million-vote increase in the two-member districts between 1962 and 1974, or just 34 percent of the increase.

the extent of the LDP's decline is less apparent. In the six districts in which the electorate showed the greatest expansion between 1971 and 1974 (Saitama, Chiba, Kanagawa, Niigata, Hiroshima, and Shizuoka), the LDP obtained 50 percent of the substantial vote increase, with its share varying widely from less than nothing in Kanagawa to 103 percent in Hiroshima. In 1974 the LDP registered percentage gains in eight of the fifteen two-member districts, a not insignificant accomplishment in view of the entry of KMT candidates in all but one of these races. In any case, the point is that the political meaning of the slight decline in aggregate LDP figures can easily be exaggerated.

In the critical two-member constituencies in 1974, what were the surprises? [47] In Chiba, Watanabe Ichitarō was picked to win but finished fourth; in Fukushima, Matsudaira Isao was the favorite but came in third in a field of four; in Gumma, Sada Ichirō was favored but was third out of five; in Kagoshima, the prospects of comeback hopeful Saigō Kichinosuke convinced the pollsters but not the voters —he wound up third out of six; in Shizuoka, Saitō Toshio was favored but ended up third; in Hiroshima, Nakazui Makoto was given a good chance to win but failed by over 100,000 votes; and in Ibaragi and Tochigi the two LDP-endorsed candidates, Kōri Yūichi and Yano Noboru, both fell short, missing the third slot by fewer than 20,000 votes. For Kōri—former leader of the LDP upper house delegation and a three-time cabinet minister—the defeat was stinging. What did all these LDP losers have in common? They were all incumbents or former upper house members; they were relatively old, averaging sixty-seven years (winners in these districts averaged fifty-three years of age); and, with two exceptions, they were ex-bureaucrats. Their common misfortune at the polls lent credence to the observation made by one LDP politician to an election night television audience: "It's just not a time for feudal lords" (*tonosama no jidai ja nai*).

The manner in which the vote of the two LDP candidates has been split has influenced past election results in the two-member districts. Since 1962 the LDP has run two candidates successfully thirteen times. [48] On six other occasions, a more even division of the LDP vote might have brought victory to both candidates. In all other cases there were simply too few total LDP votes, no matter how they might have been divided, to affect the outcome. In the past five

---

[47] The LDP candidates mentioned in this paragraph were favored by at least two major national polls.

[48] In forty-three attempts at winning both seats in House of Councillors elections since 1962, the two LDP candidates have finished in first and second place thirteen times, in first and third place seventeen times, in second and third place ten times, and in second and fourth place three times.

upper house elections the LDP has won both seats only when certain conditions have been met—when the LDP vote was divided evenly between the two LDP contenders; when the LDP faced a single opponent, its vote percentage was more than twice that of the adversary; or when, with the LDP confronting three or more opposing candidates, the opposition's percentage of the vote was distributed fairly evenly. The latter two sets of circumstances have been somewhat accidental, appearing in only three of thirteen cases.

Further, a winning LDP two-candidate strategy has not proven feasible in every two-member district. It has only worked successfully in nine of the fifteen districts of this type. And the LDP has only batted .300 when running two candidates in these constituencies. This average, furthermore, is declining: in the 1971 and 1974 elections, the LDP monopolized only one of the fifteen two-member districts.

Among all two-member districts, only in Kumamoto did the LDP secure more than 60 percent of the vote in 1974. But no possible redistribution of the LDP vote in any two-member district except Kagoshima would have altered the 1974 outcome in the LDP's favor. Ironically, opposition party (KMT-JSP) cooperation in Kumamoto probably helped dilute total opposition strength, leaving the LDP as the beneficiary, so that it picked up both seats. Except in Kumamoto, the Socialists were powerful enough to block an LDP sweep.

In the past, the most common pattern in the two-member districts has been a one-two LDP-JSP finish. In 1974 the net effect of the LDP's running two candidates in districts of marginal promise was to vault the JSP candidate into the number one position. In over half the cases—a new high—the JSP candidate placed first (although, of course, the two LDP candidates together obtained a larger percentage of the vote). Also, for the first time since 1962, the LDP's second candidate was beaten by a party other than the Socialists—by the JCP in Saitama and by the KMT in Chiba. The Kōmeitō had never before taken a seat in a two-member district, and the Communists only twice since 1962.

The scenario the LDP is most likely to face in the two-member districts in the future is one of multiple opposition candidates. The 1974 election brought Kōmeitō candidates into these contests for the first time. It was thought that the KMT might win seats in Saitama, Chiba, and Kanagawa, three crowded urban districts where the party has a large following. Even though the KMT lost in these districts (and secured only 11.5 percent of the vote in all two-member constituencies where its candidates were standing for the first time), its sizable percentage of the vote in all three districts in 1974 may pose an increasingly common dilemma for LDP campaign strategists in future elections. In Chiba, for instance, the KMT received one-fifth of the vote, the JSP one-quarter, and the JCP one-tenth. Since the two LDP candidates finished in the second and fourth positions, and the LDP second-place candidate won but 50,000 votes more than the KMT challenger, a slightly stronger KMT performance would have shut out the LDP. There was a similar configuration in Saitama, Nagano, Kyoto, and Kanagawa. The odds against the LDP's capturing both seats in these five districts in the future seem insurmountable. In fact, as in Chiba, running two candidates may spell defeat for both. A further decline in LDP vote percentages may deter the party from putting forward two candidates in any two-member district except, perhaps, the conservative strongholds of Kagoshima and Kumamoto. In the remaining "swing" two-member districts—Niigata, Okayama, Hiroshima, Shizuoka, Tochigi, Gumma, Ibaragi, and Fukushima—conditions are still uncertain and any decision will likely depend on the individual qualifications of LDP candidates, the strength of the adversary or adversaries, and the distribution of the vote. Since an enlarged KMT and JCP vote would probably come at the JSP's expense,[49] particularly in urban districts, multiple opposition candidates could prove to be a windfall for the LDP. A relatively stronger KMT and JCP might permit the LDP—if it can obtain about half the vote—to run two candidates successfully in these swing districts.

In addition to the two-member districts, the LDP in the 1974 election ran two candidates in two of the multimember districts—Hokkaido (four-member) and Fukuoka (three-member). In the other multimember districts the LDP adopted a defensive strategy, endorsing but one candidate rather than risking losing both by running two. As in many of the two-member districts, it seemed until the last votes were tabulated that the LDP might take two seats in both Hokkaido and Fukuoka. In Fukuoka, preelection surveys (*Asahi, Nikkei, Mainichi*) had indicated that LDP candidate Onimaru Katsu-yuki as well as his LDP running mate would win, but he finished fourth. In Hokkaido—the chief source of postelection LDP trauma—party strategists made a tactical mistake by running two candidates since a right-wing Seirankai-related independent (Takahashi Tatsuo) was also in the field. LDP elder statesman Kimura Takeo confessed

---

[49] Comparing 1971 and 1974 vote percentages in districts where the KMT ran candidates for the first time, the JSP percentage was off 7.5 percent, the LDP 5.4 percent, and the JCP 1 percent. *Asahi Shimbun*, 10 July 1974.

privately after the election that this had been the party's biggest blunder.[50]

The Japan Socialist Party. After the Socialists' strong showing in the 1971 election, buoyant party leaders announced that they had finally brought the downward trend in the JSP's long sagging fortunes to "a dead halt." The 1974 election results, however, made these assertions seem premature.

In the national constituency, the JSP share of the vote dropped over six percentage points from its 1971 level. Although ten of the twelve Socialist national-constituency candidates won, only three had much appeal in the metropolitan and urban areas. The distribution of the JSP's national vote (see Figure 3-4) was strikingly similar to that of the LDP. Moreover, the JSP had no big winners—contrary to what it had achieved in past national-constituency contests. In 1974 the JSP's brightest light was Meguro Kesajirō, in ninth place, who garnered only one-third as many votes as the LDP's top finisher Miyata Teru. Meguro, backed by the 480,000-member Locomotive Engineers Union, proved by his high ranking that it is still possible to win big in the national constituency with a single supporting organization, provided public interest can somehow be aroused. Meguro had become the champion of the union's slow-down program in the 1974 spring labor offensive. Besides Meguro, both Socialist candidates representing the million-member Jichirō won, as did both from Nikkyōso. Jichirō- and Nikkyōso-backed candidates secured more votes (1.38 million and 1.26 million respectively) than in the past three elections. Overall, JSP labor union candidates received 80 percent of the JSP national-constituency vote. The two JSP losers in the national constituency had diffuse and lukewarm public support and weak supporting organizations.

In the local constituencies, the JSP—"scissored" by a strengthened JCP and the entry of KMT candidates—took eleven fewer seats and five percentage points less of the vote than in 1971. For the first time ever, the party was shut out completely in the one-member districts and, even though it won more seats in the two-member districts than in the previous election, it succeeded mainly in protecting what it already had. Further, except in Kagoshima and Kumamoto, the JSP vote percentage dropped in all two-member districts, and by a full 10 percent in five of these districts. Its gains in Kuma-

---

[50] Interview with the author, 12 July 1974. After all, the LDP had received only 40 percent of the Hokkaido vote in the 1972 lower house election. See Curtis, pp. 71-72, for details on the Hokkaido campaign.

moto stemmed from KMT cooperation, and the slight improvement in its performance in the four-member districts was aided by the LDP's tactical error in Hokkaido.

Having touted their party as the "party of the floating vote" and "the vanguard of the progressives," the JSP leaders watched stunned as it dropped to fourth place in the cities, with its share of the urban vote plummeting by ten percentage points from its level in the preceding election.[51] The party failed to win a single seat in two three-member urban districts, Osaka and Hyogo. It was the disastrous showing in the cities that sparked a fierce postelection debate within the JSP over future prospects. After all, the party not only failed to attract the floating vote and to advance in the urban areas, it declined in rural districts and was barely able to hold its traditional Sōhyō support base. But of the winning JSP candidates, 75 percent were labor-related, as against 64 percent in 1971. The JSP's feeble attempt to broaden its electoral base beyond Sōhyō failed, and the results merely reaffirmed the prevailing impression of the JSP as the "Sōhyō party."

One reason for the relatively poor JSP showing, of course, was the entry of KMT candidates into the local-constituency contests. Although precise figures are unavailable, much of the KMT vote in these races evidently came at the expense of the JSP. Further, the Socialists were supposed to have been weakened by KMT and JCP inroads into traditionally JSP unions, though this does not show up clearly in the data.

In sum, the JSP and the LDP face similar problems. Both have weakening support among the public and the organizations that have traditionally supported them. Both are losing votes to the other parties, especially in the A- and B-type districts. Both have lackluster images and are plagued by intraparty feuds.

In view of the JSP's frequently stated goal of leading the opposition parties to victory over the conservatives in 1974, its defensive campaign is rather curious. In a sense the party lost by not trying to win. Its dull and uninspired campaign failed to capture the popular imagination. Before the election a *Mainichi* survey asked: "Is there a party you would absolutely not vote for?" and only 12 percent responded, "the JSP," the lowest percentage scored by any party.[52] The JSP has not aroused dislike so much as disinterest.

---

[51] From 21.5 to 11.6 percent, using national-constituency figures.

[52] *Mainichi Shimbun,* 22 June 1974. Moreover, the JSP has become middle-aged— its strongest supporters, previously in their twenties and thirties, are now in their forties.

The Japan Communist Party. By some indicators, the Communist performance in the 1974 election was impressive. The JCP's attempts to broaden its base of support into new sectors were more successful than those of any other party—its strategy of running lawyers, teachers, and doctors produced 41 percent of the JCP winners; its five women candidates gained higher vote percentages than the men, and two were winners; and its effort to expand Communist strength outside the cities was effective. Communist candidates obtained 42.5 percent more local-constituency votes than in 1971, and 53 percent more in the rural and semi-rural (D- and E-type) prefectural districts. The JCP's defeats were modest and were confined to six prefectures. Some of its successes, on the other hand, were spectacular: in Hokkaido the Communist candidate (a woman) garnered nearly 200,000 votes more than the JCP had received in 1971.[53] The urban-rural distribution of the Communist local-constituency vote remained relatively unchanged, though the party came out of the election slightly less dependent upon the urban vote than it had previously been. (See Figure 3-4.)

But the generally favorable 1974 JCP performance was qualified in several respects. To begin with, the party was not as strong as expected in the national constituency. The JCP's concentration on building up its nonurban base may have hurt its candidates assigned to urban districts. A last minute reassignment of designated districts was needed to push two borderline candidates above the winning line. Another hindrance may have lain in the fact that six of the eight Communist national candidates were running for the first time. Furthermore, while the party gained in votes and seats, it did not substantially raise its share of the overall vote (up just 1.3 percentage points) in the national constituency. Nor did the party draw more than 10 to 15 percent of the swollen floating vote, which seemed to go mostly to the independents. In fact, while there is still room for the party to expand in the rural areas, it may have already peaked in the cities.[54] Also, because the JCP national-constituency vote fell half a million votes beneath its 1972 general election total, the party will likely have to work hard in the next general election just to maintain its present position.[55] Finally, although the party softened the tone of

---

[53] Figures from *Akahata*, 9 July 1974.

[54] The Communist share of the metropolitan vote in 1974 was 13.5 percent, up less than two-tenths of one percentage point from 1971.

[55] The apparent pattern in JCP election strategy has been to use the party's total vote as the minimum goal for the upper house national constituency and then to use the latter as the basis for the next lower house election, and so forth. The JCP received nearly 5.5 million votes in the 1972 general election and, given

its position statements in 1974,[56] there continues to be strong anti-JCP feeling among the public and the other parties, sentiments that will be exacerbated by Communist gains. In the *Mainichi* poll cited earlier, 42 percent of those interviewed asserted they would never vote Communist—far more than refused to vote for any other party.[57] The party's intransigent approach toward cooperation with the other minority parties may prove an obstacle to mounting joint campaigns and to broadening the JCP base in the future.

Kōmeitō. The election results showed that the KMT had been unable to expand its base beyond Sōka Gakkai. Every non-Gakkai KMT candidate in the local constituencies lost. Every one of the party's fourteen winners (nine national, five local) had had Gakkai experience. In the national constituency, the KMT received more votes in 1974 than in 1971 but obtained less than 6 percent of the 12.6 million additional votes cast in 1974. Moreover, the KMT share of the vote dropped in all district types—A through E. In the national contest, the KMT was aided slightly by the decision of a Shinsanbetsu (National Federation of Industrial Organizations) union to recommend one KMT candidate, an unprecedented action. Party officials hailed this as the opening wedge for the KMT in organized labor, an opening that could be widened to embrace small- and medium-sized businesses and as yet unorganized working groups.

In the prefectural contests, despite scattered gains in metropolitan and urban areas, the party gained only a small fraction more total votes than it did in the national constituency—suggesting that individual KMT candidates had limited popular appeal. Like those gained by the JCP, the seats and votes won by the KMT in the local constituencies were mostly at the expense of the JSP.

Although the KMT was frustrated in its attempt to build its national base, its inner core of support is more solid than that of any other Japanese political party.[58] Polls show that KMT supporters,

---

the projected winning threshold of 550,000 votes for a national candidate and the increase in public support for the JCP, it was thought that ten candidates were possible. It was this reasoning that led many observers to be surprised when the party ran only eight. The weak showing in 1974 may cause Communist party leaders to lower their sights for the next general election.

[56] When the writer asked a prominent *Asahi* political analyst why the Communists had all of a sudden become so moderate and respectable, he was told, "Be serious, they want to win, don't they?"

[57] *Mainichi Shimbun*, 22 June 1974.

[58] For a useful contrast of KMT, JSP, and JCP effectiveness in controlling votes in the 1971 election, see Nishihira Shigeki, *Nihon no senkyo* (Tokyo: Shiseidō, 1972), pp. 173–175.

more than those of any other party, vote for the party rather than the candidate.[59] The number of KMT votes in the 1974 national constituency going to nondesignated candidates—what might be termed "slippage"—was less than the JCP's slippage. A remarkable 92 percent of the national KMT vote went to KMT-backed candidates. By contrast, the percentage of properly controlled votes for the JCP was 83.5.[60] The KMT has a stable political base.

But slippage figures have another dimension: they give some indication of the degree of party appeal to the floating vote. Presumably, non-KMT voters are less likely than party members to know the party-designated candidate. The low KMT slippage rate would suggest that the party failed to win much of the floating vote. By comparison, the JCP's high percentage of misdirected national-constituency votes implies a somewhat greater appeal to the uncommitted voter.

The Democratic Socialist Party. Since losing two of their top leaders by death and retirement several years ago, the Democratic Socialists have performed dismally in national elections. The 1974 election did nothing to brighten the DSP outlook. The heavy turnout brought the party more votes than in 1971, but the DSP's share of the increase stayed about the same as its portion of the overall vote (4 to 5 percent). Only five DSP candidates were winners—four national and one local—barely enough to retain for the party its right to introduce legislation in the parliament and not enough to restore the flagging spirits of DSP supporters.

The DSP ran a nonlabor candidate in the national constituency in the 1974 election, a tentative move toward expanding its base. But all the DSP winners in the national constituency were from Dōmei-affiliated unions. The party's star national performer, Tabuchi Tetsuya, had the support of the 900,000-member Automobile Workers Union and the enthusiastic backing of Nissan factory workers. Tabuchi received nearly 60 percent of his vote in factory areas.[61] But Dōmei support was not enough to make DSP candidates winners in the local constituencies.

The only DSP local winner was a former bureaucrat who had held an administrative vice-ministership in the Ministry of Labor—Sanji Shigenobu, in three-member Aichi Prefecture. The party's

[59] For example, *Mainichi Shimbun*, 22 June 1974.
[60] JCP slippage in the semi-rural and rural (D- and E-type) districts rose dramatically from 1971 and seems to show the looseness of the party's organizational structure in these areas.
[61] *Sankei Shimbun*, 10 July 1974.

Table 3-7

DSP SHARE OF TOTAL NATIONAL-CONSTITUENCY VOTE
BY DISTRICT TYPE (DEGREE OF URBANIZATION), HOUSE
OF COUNCILLORS ELECTIONS, 1968, 1971, AND 1974

(in percents)

District Type	1968	1971	1974
A Metropolitan	7.53	7.65	6.66
B Urban	7.06	6.69	6.39
C Semi-urban	4.81	5.50	5.62
D Semi-rural	5.09	4.84	5.18
E Rural	3.53	3.87	4.44

Sources: Author's calculations based on statistics from the Ministry of Home Affairs and the Central Election Management Committee.

difficulties are typified by Sanji's campaign. Three factors were intertwined in Sanji's victory: good Dōmei support (Toyota's main plant is located in Aichi); his skill at courting conservative support among business management, agriculture, and religious sectors, all the while playing down his official DSP connection; and the fact that only one LDP candidate was running, which enlarged his potential constituency among Aichi conservatives. Sanji's adroit juggling of the conservatives and progressives, and of labor and management—in a favorable election environment—gave him the win. He finished in second place with a fifth of the vote.

Sanji's campaign suggests the nature of the DSP's identity problem. A survey conducted before the July election showed that most people (including DSP supporters) were uncertain as to whether the party was conservative or progressive.[62] Party support among labor union members has been dwindling, and the party's policy of "cooperating both with labor and management" (rōshi kyōchō) seems to have satisfied no one. Moreover, national-constituency figures for the past three elections show a gradual drift of DSP support away from the urban areas.[63] Table 3-7 makes this apparent.

Neither conservative nor progressive, fully affiliated neither with labor nor with management, the DSP would seem to have an opportunity to carve out a moderate centrist place for itself in a society that extols middle-of-the-road compromise and denigrates polarized

[62] *Mainichi Shimbun*, 22 June 1974.
[63] See Figure 3-4.

politics and intransigent confrontations. It was perhaps thinking along this line that motivated DSP election strategy in 1974—to seek a party identity beyond Dōmei, to occupy the middle ground, equidistant between the conservatives and the progressives. But a centrist party has never done well in Japanese politics, in part because the middle ground is vulnerable, open to attack from all sides. Moreover, the DSP leadership, national organization, support base, and Diet representation are too enfeebled to enable the party to plunge ahead on its own. Instead, its very frailty will force the DSP to work with others and makes it fearful of being swallowed up by other far stronger parties. The only DSP option seems to be to serve as a bridge or broker between the conservatives and the progressives, a role made possible by the ebbing of LDP strength and the relative gains of the more progressive parties—the KMT and the JCP. Thus, the DSP's weakness may prove paradoxically to be a source of strength, giving the party political leverage far beyond that derived from its ten seats in the House of Councillors.

Implications

What was the 1974 House of Councillors election all about? In many respects the 1974 election was "about" the fundamental political issues of any free democratic society: the exercise of power, the rights of minorities, the freedom of unencumbered choice, and appropriate campaign behavior. In a world in which the number of authoritarian and controlled societies continues to grow, it is encouraging that the long-term impact of the 1974 election seemed, however hesitantly, to be in the direction of extending the boundaries of individual political freedom. The political underpinnings of the Japanese democratic system were tested in this election, and it was the very freedom of the system that permitted such experimentation to take place. Several companies sought to manipulate the votes of their employees but their attempts proved ineffective. "Japan, Inc." was stopped short of the ballot box. The 1974 election also showed that the unique national constituency continues to provide a means of representation for many special interest groups and a few places in the House of Councillors for candidates armed only with ideals.[64]

It seems clear that Japan is entering an era in which lines of political loyalty will not be as tightly drawn as in the past. Weakening political loyalties and loosening traditional support structures will make Japanese politics more fragmented and fluid than in the past.

---

[64] See Passin, pp. 26-33.

One can expect that this trend toward fragmentation will continue and perhaps accelerate, given the pronounced tendency of the younger generation toward disaffection with politics and political parties. Assuming the continuation of present trends, in ten years the Japanese electorate may be split into three roughly equal "camps": those who support the conservative LDP, those who favor the progressive parties, and those without political party affiliation or preferences. This "three-party" system would have serious implications for each political party and the future direction of Japanese politics, as indeed it would for the course of American politics.

The Prospects for the Opposition. In this emerging situation, there are limits on the ability of any one opposition party to expand much beyond its current levels of public support or existing political support structures. Each party will have to accept competition. This may be difficult, since the 1974 election suggested that one opposition party's gain tends to be another opposition party's loss.

Only far in the future, given current trends, will any single opposition party be able to build the national support structure necessary to challenge the LDP for the authority to govern Japan. In the meantime, cooperation of some sort between and among the opposition parties is the only avenue by which the opposition can feasibly pursue its aspirations to leadership.

The acid test of cooperation has always been the extent to which any party will sacrifice its own political interests in a national election. By this standard, cooperation in the 1974 campaign was illusory. What was advertised as cooperation—party officials stumping jointly, party workers distributing literature and hanging posters for candidates of other parties—was unenthusiastic. "Cooperation" was actually no more than a temporary truce for the duration of the election, an expedient motivated by the negative goal of blocking the LDP, not by a genuine or positive spirit of cooperation. The opposition parties joined forces only where one of them had nothing to lose. The KMT, for instance, backed JSP candidates only in districts where KMT support was low in any event, as in the one-member districts.[65] Except in Okinawa, cooperation failed to produce a single opposition victory—either in the five districts where there was formal cooperation or in the six one-member districts where the KMT lent its informal support to Socialist candidates.

---

[65] The KMT did not run candidates in Ishikawa, Fukui, Shimane, Fukushima, or Kagawa, or in districts where there was opposition cooperation. In all of these districts the party's support rate was less than 5 percent and the KMT had never received more than 10 percent of the national-constituency vote.

The JSP-KMT joint campaign in Kumamoto, a two-member conservative district in Kyushu, points to the frustrations of cooperative campaigns. In the spring the KMT organization in Kumamoto agreed, by a narrow seventeen-vote margin, to back the Socialist candidate, Matsumae Tatsurō. Matsumae, the president of Tōkai University, aided his cause by paying personal visits to KMT prefectural offices, and the KMT secretary-general helped by going to Kumamoto in late June to persuade reluctant party members to line up behind Matsumae. Besides receiving KMT assistance, calculated at 50–60,000 votes, and the backing of the local Sōhyō organization, Matsumae was thought to appeal to the floating vote and the intellectuals. Given a winning-line projection of 240,000 votes and 150,000 hard-core JSP votes, Kumamoto seemed to present a possible victory for the opposition. Even with substantial KMT support in the election,[66] however, the high voting rate (81 percent) and the near-perfect split of the LDP's vote between its two contenders brought Matsumae down. Perhaps a three-way JCP-JSP-KMT cooperative strategy could have succeeded, but antipathy toward the Communists from both KMT and JSP members might still have driven votes to the LDP. The main lesson of Kumamoto and of the opposition cooperative program in general is that the votes of any one party cannot simply be transferred to another by administrative fiat without considerable slippage.

Further, a united front strategy is not always the proper solution. Had the opposition parties cooperated in Hokkaido, for example, the LDP, instead of winning nothing, would have captured one or possibly two seats.[67] The number of districts where opposition teamwork can work is limited.

For the future, each opposition party has a Hobson's choice: follow a united-front path with the risk of losing its individual party identity but with an increased chance of winning, or go it alone, building an independent political base (jitsuryoku kyōka) but with diminished prospects of victory. Winning will require cooperation that may weaken each party's individual character (dokujisei) and sense of identity (seitōkan).

---

[66] Exact figures are unavailable, but it seems that at least several thousand Kōmeitō supporters in Kumamoto voted Communist since the JCP received roughly 3,000 fewer votes from this district in the national constituency than in the local. Nevertheless, the KMT was apparently the most reliable "cooperator" in 1974. Perhaps JSP voters are more likely allies of the Communists than of the KMT, for it appears that a larger percentage of the Socialist vote went to the JCP in Kochi than to the KMT in Wakayama.

[67] This is explained in Curtis, pp. 71-72.

In 1974 the Japan Socialist party, confident from its 1971 showing, failed to work hard enough to achieve cooperation. Despite the disappointing JSP performance in the election, however, the JSP continues to be the strongest of the opposition parties and will be at the center of any future cooperative campaign ventures. The KMT straddled the issue in 1974, joining in selected cooperative campaigns with the JSP while flooding the local districts with new candidates to build up KMT strength for future elections. Another cooperative approach is all-opposition support of an independent candidate, as in Kanagawa and Okinawa. But this also merely circumvents the key issue: how to retain a separate party identity while searching out and exploiting potential areas of common interest. There are islands of political and ideological mutuality among the progressives, but these were not linked effectively at election time. Nor did the 1974 election resolve the conflict among the three main opposition parties over leadership of the progressive camp.

The lesson that the progressives ought to have learned from the 1974 election is that they can win more votes the less heavily they are freighted with ideology. If this lesson has been learned, it may be that future opposition party interests, goals, and methods will be more moderate and attuned more closely to public concerns. There may also be a greater sensitivity to the needs of new groups and sectors, as Japanese politics moves into an era where multiple support structures are mandatory for success in national elections.

The Need for a New Conservative Course. The LDP, the party that is supposedly impervious to change, has already changed. It has sought to appeal to new and different constituencies by endorsing different candidates, such as the *tarento*. Most observers were dismayed by certain features of the 1974 LDP campaign—its reliance on local politicians, "enterprise" candidates, and PR manipulation— but these did at least reflect the party's willingness to be flexible. Even though there had been corporate-backed candidates in the past, the "joining of politics and finance" (*zaisei ippon*) to the degree achieved in 1974 was a major departure in Japanese election politics, with profound implications for the future. The frustration and anger of some LDP business supporters following the election, manifested in the demand made by a disillusioned few that party factions be abolished, stemmed from the LDP's inability to capture the predicted number of seats in the election and from a belief that Tanaka's no-holds-barred campaign style had tarnished the party's image both in Japan and abroad. Nonetheless, any dramatic shift away from past

LDP campaign practices or a sudden withering of traditional LDP financial sources is highly unlikely. The business community (*zaikai*) has been the linchpin of postwar support for the LDP. "Cabinets come and go," the saying goes, "but the *zaikai* is the 10,000-year party in power." LDP politicians will continue to turn to big business for funds in future election campaigns. No easy answers emerged from the 1974 campaign, but the election tested the permissible outer limits of electioneering in Japan. For the conservative LDP, the main lesson of 1974 was perhaps that it went too far both in equating the party's absolute majority in the Diet and perpetuation in office with the survival of a free society, and in its vast expenditures of money, energy, and time to prove the point. Some excessive and unsuccessful approaches will in the future seem less attractive than they did in 1974 and may be discarded. In addition to the salutary effect this election may have upon campaign practices, one may argue, though with sagging conviction, that in future LDP campaigns more attention will be given to the conflict of ideas than to stratagems and wiles.

Resilience has been one reason for the LDP's past domination of Japanese politics. The party structure houses diverse elements—bureaucrats, businessmen, organizational representatives, local politicians—with contending but essentially compatible interests. The LDP retains broad-based public appeal, a generally effective administrative organization, and the financial support of prominent business organizations. It is still the only Japanese political party that approaches most issues from a national perspective. Its relatively weak performance in the 1974 election is misleading. It was on the offensive throughout the campaign. It set the issues of the campaign. It adroitly took over the opposition's main campaign weapon, *hokaku gyakuten* or "reversal of the conservatives and the progressives," and used it effectively to its own advantage.[68] The weak LDP performance resulted from an accumulation of small tactical disadvantages and miscalculations—though, to be sure, public support for the LDP has diminished slightly in certain sectors and districts.

The LDP's task is to shore up its rural base while attracting urban voters. It has hitherto been more successful in the national constituency than the local, and its supporters can take some solace from the fact that it has been more adept at base-building and appealing to new organizations and segments of the population than the opposition parties—except, of course, the JCP.

It would be premature to project a sharp decline for the LDP on the basis of the 1974 election results alone. Events since the upper

---

[68] See Curtis, pp. 46-47.

house contest suggest that Prime Minister Miki Takeo is more willing than his immediate predecessor to seek to bridge the sometimes yawning abyss that has separated the LDP from its "progressive" adversaries. The party did well in the 1975 local elections and is expected to score modest gains at the opposition's expense in the 1976 lower house election. Nonetheless, the longer-term trend of LDP decline is unmistakable and does underscore the party's need to unify its somewhat fragmented support structure and to chart a new conservative course. The party will have to open new areas of popular appeal, especially since the Japanese voter is far less sympathetic than in the past to the conservatives. Party leaders in particular believe the LDP needs a new image, that of an action-oriented party willing to take firm positions on the substance as well as the trappings of policy. While the LDP is in no danger of immediate demise, its response to the lessons of the 1974 House of Councillors election is far more important than the results themselves. And in this process, many LDP leaders would urge the party to take seriously its own slogan from the 1974 campaign: "now is the time to do it!" (*yarubeki toki wa ima!*).

APPENDIX
Statistical Data

Compiled by the authors
with the assistance of Nobuo Tomita

Table A-1

AVERAGE AGE OF CANDIDATES FOR 1971 AND 1974
HOUSE OF COUNCILLORS ELECTIONS, BY PARTY,
NATIONAL AND LOCAL CONSTITUENCIES
(in percentages of total candidates)

	Party					Average of All Parties
	LDP	JSP	KMT	DSP	JCP	
National constituency						
1971	57.4	53.1	48.5	47.7	64.8	53.9
1974	57.7	55.0	46.4	53.8	50.1	53.8
Local constituencies						
1971	60.9	52.9	40.0	49.2	47.5	52.9
1974	59.9	51.5	42.5	47.0	46.3	51.7

Source: Adapted from *Yomiuri Shimbun,* 18 June 1974.

Table A-2

OCCUPATION AND STATUS OF CANDIDATES,[a] 1974 HOUSE OF COUNCILLORS ELECTION

	National Constituency				Local Constituencies				Total
	Incumbent	Former incumbent candidate	New candidate	Sub-total	Incumbent	Former incumbent candidate	New candidate	Sub-total	
Ex-bureaucrats	8	—	4	12	12	—	6	18	30 (10.6)
Labor	5	—	10	15	7	—	21	28	43 (15.2)
"Talent"	3	—	8	11	—	—	2	2	13 (4.6)
Party workers	4	—	3	7	2	—	32	34	41 (14.5)
Prefectural governors and vice-governors	—	1	—	0	3	1	9	13	13 (4.6)
Prefectural assemblymen	4	1	1	6	8	—	41	49	55 (19.4)
Self-employed	4	—	9	13	3	—	22	25	38 (13.4)
Business-related	3	1	5	9	7	1	11	19	28 (9.9)
Other	3	1	—	4	4	1	13	18	22 (7.8)
Total	34	3	40	77	46	3	157	206	283 (100.0)

a Excludes "bubble" candidates, those candidates not having any chance of getting elected (see Curtis, p. 57).

Source: Adapted from Fuji Telecasting Company, *Documents for the 10th Upper House Election,* 7 July 1974.

Table A-3

NUMBER OF NEW, INCUMBENT, AND FORMER INCUMBENT CANDIDATES, BY PARTY, 1974 HOUSE OF COUNCILLORS ELECTION

| | Party | | | | | | | |
	LDP	JSP	KMT	JCP	DSP	MIN	IND	**Totals**
National constituency								
Incumbents	14	6	8	2	2	0	2	34
Former incumbents	2	0	0	0	0	0	1	3
New candidates	19	6	1	6	3	5	35	75
Subtotals	35	12	9	8	5	5	38	112
Local constituencies								
Incumbents	31	7	3	2	1	0	2	46
Former incumbents	3	0	0	0	0	0	0	3
New candidates	26	38	33	43	8	6	34	188
Subtotals	60	45	36	45	9	6	36	237
Totals	95	57	45	53	14	11	74	349

Source: Based on Ministry of Home Affairs data.

Table A-4

NUMBER OF CANDIDATES, NUMBER AND PERCENTAGE OF SEATS WON, NUMBER OF VOTES AND PERCENTAGE OF TOTAL VOTE, BY PARTY, HOUSE OF COUNCILLORS ELECTIONS, 1947–1974

1947

	National Constituency			Local Constituencies			All Constituencies	
	Candidates	Votes	Candidates elected	Candidates	Votes	Candidates elected	Candidates	Candidates elected
Liberal party (Jiyūtō)	18	1,360,456 6.4%	8 8.0%	54	3,769,704 17.1%	30 20.0%	72	38 15.2%
Democratic party (Minshūtō)	13	1,508,087 7.1%	6 6.0%	41	2,989,132 13.6%	22 14.6%	54	28 11.2%
Socialist party (Shakaitō)	33	3,479,814 16.3%	17 17.0%	66	4,901,341 22.2%	30 20.0%	99	47 18.8%
Communist party (Kyōsantō)	12	610,948 2.9%	3 3.0%	28	825,304 3.8%	1 0.7%	40	4 1.6%
Minor parties	30	1,613,169 7.6%	9 9.0%	29	2,036,554 9.2%	13 8.7%	59	22 8.8%
Independents	140	12,698,698 59.7%	57 57.0%	113	7,527,191 34.1%	54 36.0%	253	111 44.4%
Totals	246	21,271,172 100.0%	100 100.0%	331	22,049,226 100.0%	150 100.0%	577	250 100.0%

1950

Party								
Liberal party (Jiyūtō)	73	8,313,756 29.7%	18 32.1%	63	10,414,995 35.9%	34 44.8%	136	52 39.4%
Nat'l Dem. party (Kokumin Minshutō)	18	1,368,783 4.9%	1 1.8%	28	2,966,011 10.2%	8 10.5%	46	9 6.8%
Socialist party (Shakaitō)	32	4,854,629 17.3%	15 26.8%	43	7,316,808 25.2%	21 27.7%	75	36 27.3%
Communist party (Kyōsantō)	12	1,333,872 4.8%	2 3.6%	38	1,637,451 5.7%	0	50	2 1.5%
Green Breeze Society (Ryokufūkai)	40	3,660,391 13.1%	6 10.7%	18	1,773,576 6.1%	3 3.9%	58	9 6.8%
Minor parties	19	829,436 2.9%	2 3.6%	23	1,430,142 4.9%	3 3.9%	42	5 3.8%
Independents	117	7,632,526 27.3%	12 21.4%	39	3,465,956 12.0%	7 9.2%	156	19 14.4%
Totals	311	27,998,393 100.0%	56 100.0%	252	29,004,939 100.0%	76 100.0%	563	132 100.0%

1953

Party								
Hatoyama [a] Liberal party	1	110,889 0.4%	0	7	522,540 1.9%	0	8	0
Yoshida Liberal [b] party	38	6,149,927 22.8%	16 30.1%	45	3,803,131 31.4%	30 40.0%	83	46 35.9%
Reform party (Kaishintō)	17	1,630,507 6.0%	3 5.7%	26	2,840,345 10.1%	5 6.7%	43	8 6.3%
Left Socialist party	24	3,858,552 14.3%	8 15.1%	26	3,917,837 14.0%	10 13.3%	50	18 14.0%

Table A-4 (continued)

	National Constituency			Local Constituencies			All Constituencies	
	Candidates	Votes	Candidates elected	Candidates	Votes	Candidates elected	Candidates	Candidates elected
Right Socialist party	15	1,740,423 6.4%	3 5.7%	24	2,952,803 10.5%	7 9.3%	39	10 7.8%
Communist party (Kyōsantō)	3	293,887 1.1%	0	9	264,729 0.9%	0	12	0
Green Breeze Society (Ryokufūkai)	22	3,301,011 12.2%	8 15.1%	12	2,096,103 7.5%	8 10.7%	34	16 12.5%
Minor parties	12	445,433 1.6%	0	6	600,116 2.2%	1 1.3%	18	1 0.8%
Independents	102	9,504,220 35.2%	15 28.3%	58	6,013,363 21.5%	14 18.7%	160	29 22.7%
Totals	234	27,034,839 100.0%	53 100.0%	213	28,010,967 100.0%	75 100.0%	447	128 100.0%

a Refers to conservative group led by Hatoyama Ichirō.
b Refers to major conservative party wing under Yoshida Shigeru.

1956

	National Constituency			Local Constituencies			All Constituencies	
Liberal Democratic party (Jiyū Minshutō)	54	11,356,874 39.7%	19 36.5%	64	14,353,960 48.4%	42 56.0%	118	61 48.0%
Socialist party (Shakaitō)	29	8,549,989 29.9%	21 40.3%	53	11,156,060 37.6%	28 37.3%	82	49 38.6%

	National constituency			Local constituency			Total	
Communist party (Kyōsantō)	3	599,253 / 2.1%	1 / 2.0%	31	1,149,009 / 3.9%	1 / 1.3%	34	2 / 1.6%
Green Breeze Society (Ryokufūkai)	14	2,877,101 / 10.1%	5 / 9.6%	5	653,843 / 2.2%	0	19	5 / 3.9%
Minor parties	10	789,356 / 2.7%	1 / 2.0%	10	236,276 / 0.8%	0	20	1 / 0.8%
Independents	40	4,433,885 / 15.5%	5 / 9.6%	28	2,136,498 / 7.1%	4 / 5.4%	68	9 / 7.1%
Totals	150	28,616,411 / 100.0%	52 / 100.0%	191	29,685,646 / 100.0%	75 / 100.0%	341	127 / 100.0%

1959

	National constituency			Local constituency			Total	
Liberal Democratic party (Jiyū Minshutō)	36	12,120,597 / 41.2%	22 / 42.3%	65	15,667,021 / 52.0%	49 / 65.3%	101	71 / 55.9%
Socialist party (Shakaitō)	25	7,794,753 / 26.5%	17 / 32.7%	53	10,265,393 / 34.1%	21 / 28.0%	78	38 / 29.9%
Communist party (Kyōsantō)	2	551,915 / 1.9%	1 / 1.9%	34	999,255 / 3.3%	0	36	1 / 0.8%
Green Breeze Society (Ryokufūkai)	5	2,382,703 / 8.1%	4 / 7.7%	7	731,383 / 2.4%	2 / 2.7%	12	6 / 4.7%
Minor parties	10	753,261 / 2.5%	1 / 1.9%	13	155,189 / 0.5%	0	23	1 / 0.8%
Independents	44	5,817,187 / 19.8%	7 / 13.5%	36	2,311,112 / 7.7%	3 / 4.0%	80	10 / 7.9%
Totals	122	29,420,418 / 100.0%	52 / 100.0%	208	30,129,354 / 100.0%	75 / 100.0%	330	127 / 100.0%

Table A-4 (continued)

1962

	National Constituency			Local Constituencies			All Constituencies	
	Candidates	Votes	Candidates elected	Candidates	Votes	Candidates elected	Candidates	Candidates elected
Liberal Democratic party (Jiyū Minshutō)	39	16,581,636 46.4%	21 41.2%	61	17,112,986 47.1%	48 63.3%	100	69 54.3%
Socialist party (Shakaitō)	19	8,666,909 24.3%	15 29.4%	50	11,917,674 32.8%	22 28.9%	69	37 29.2%
Democratic Socialist party (Minshatō)	5	1,899,756 5.3%	3 5.9%	19	2,649,422 7.3%	1 1.3%	24	4 3.2%
Clean Politics League (Kōmei Seiji Renmei)	7	4,124,269 11.5%	7 13.7%	2	958,176 2.6%	2 2.6%	9	9 7.3%
Communist party (Kyōsantō)	2	1,123,946 3.1%	2 3.9%	45	1,760,257 4.8%	1 1.3%	47	3 2.2%
Comrades Association (Dōshikai)	5	1,660,465 4.7%	2 3.9%	1	128,834 0.4%	0	6	2 1.6%
Minor parties	7	295,602 0.8%	0	6	58,621 0.2%	0	13	0
Independents	23	1,404,048 3.9%	1 2.0%	37	1,725,947 4.8%	2 2.6%	60	3 2.2%
Totals	107	35,756,634 100.0%	51 100.0%	221	36,311,922 100.0%	76 100.0%	328	127 100.0%

1 9 6 5

Party								
Liberal Democratic party (Jiyū Minshutō)	36	17,583,490 47.2%	25 48.2%	59	16,651,284 44.2%	46 61.4%	95	71 55.9%
Socialist party (Shakaitō)	16	8,729,655 24.3%	12 23.1%	50	12,346,650 32.8%	24 32.0%	66	36 28.3%
Democratic Socialist party (Minshatō)	5	2,214,375 5.9%	2 3.8%	16	2,303,860 6.1%	1 1.3%	21	3 2.4%
Clean Government party (Kōmeitō)	9	5,097,682 13.7%	9 17.3%	5	1,910,975 5.1%	2 2.7%	14	11 8.6%
Communist party (Kyōsantō)	2	1,652,363 4.4%	2 3.8%	46	2,608,771 6.9%	1 1.3%	48	3 2.4%
Minor parties	9	298,400 0.8%	0	27	185,990 0.5%	0	36	0
Independents	22	1,700,848 4.6%	2 3.8%	30	1,664,639 4.4%	1 1.3%	52	3 2.4%
Totals	99	37,276,815 100.0%	52 100.0%	233	37,672,170 100.0%	75 100.0%	332	127 100.0%

1 9 6 8

Party								
Liberal Democratic party (Jiyū Minshutō)	34	20,120,089 46.7%	21 41.2%	59	19,405,545 44.9%	48 64.0%	93	69 54.7%
Socialist party (Shakaitō)	15	8,542,199 19.8%	12 23.5%	47	12,617,680 29.2%	16 21.4%	62	28 22.2%
Democratic Socialist party (Minshatō)	4	2,578,580 6.0%	4 7.8%	12	3,010,089 6.9%	3 4.0%	16	7 5.6%
Clean Government party (Kōmeitō)	9	6,656,771 15.4%	9 17.7%	5	2,632,528 6.1%	4 5.3%	14	13 10.3%

Table A-4 (continued)

	National Constituency			Local Constituencies			All Constituencies	
	Candidates	Votes	Candidates elected	Candidates	Votes	Candidates elected	Candidates	Candidates elected
Communist party (Kyōsantō)	3	2,146,878 5.0%	3 5.9%	46	3,577,179 8.3%	1 1.3%	49	4 3.2%
Minor parties	7	157,500 0.4%	0	8	106,587 0.2%	0	15	0
Independents	21	2,872,278 6.7%	2 3.9%	35	1,910,371 4.4%	3 4.0%	56	5 4.0%
Totals	93	43,074,297 100.0%	51 100.0%	212	43,259,979 100.0%	75 100.0%	305	126 100.0%
1971 c								
Liberal Democratic party (Jiyū Minshutō)	34	17,759,395 44.4%	21 42.0%	59	17,727,263 43.9%	41 54.7%	93	62 49.6%
Socialist party (Shakaitō)	13	8,494,264 21.3%	11 22.0%	47	12,597,644 31.2%	28 37.3%	60	39 31.2%
Democratic Socialist party (Minshatō)	4	2,441,508 6.1%	4 8.0%	7	1,919,643 4.8%	2 2.7%	11	6 4.8%
Clean Government party (Kōmeitō)	8	5,626,292 14.1%	8 16.0%	2	1,391,855 3.5%	2 2.7%	10	10 8.0%
Communist party (Kyōsantō)	5	3,219,306 8.1%	5 10.0%	46	4,878,570 12.1%	1 1.3%	51	6 4.8%

Minor parties	3	48,299 / 0.1%	0	6	74,739 / 0.1%	0	9	0
Independents	39	2,342,516 / 5.9%	1 / 2.0%	32	1,741,201 / 4.3%	1 / 1.3%	71	2 / 1.6%
Totals	106	39,931,583 / 100.0%	50 / 100.0%	199	40,330,915 / 100.0%	75 / 100.0%	305	125 / 100.0%

c Okinawa is not included in the 1971 calculations.

1974

Liberal Democratic party (Jiyū Minshutō)	35	23,332,773 / 44.3%	19 / 35.2%	60	21,132,372 / 39.5%	43 / 56.6%	95	62
Socialist party (Shakaitō)	12	7,990,456 / 15.2%	10 / 18.5%	45	13,907,864 / 26.0%	18 / 23.7%	57	28
Democratic Socialist party (Minshatō)	5	3,114,895 / 5.9%	4 / 7.4%	9	2,353,397 / 4.4%	1 / 1.3%	14	5
Clean Government party (Kōmeitō)	9	6,360,419 / 12.1%	9 / 16.7%	36	6,732,937 / 12.6%	5 / 6.6%	45	14
Communist party (Kyōsantō)	8	4,931,649 / 9.4%	8 / 14.8%	45	6,428,919 / 12.0%	5 / 6.6%	53	13
Minor parties	5	74,345 / 0.1%	0	6	332,716 / 0.6%	1 / 1.3%	11	1
Independents	38	6,820,199 / 13.0%	4 / 7.4%	36	2,609,195 / 4.9%	3 / 3.9%	74	7
Totals	112	52,624,736 / 100.0%	54 / 100.0%	237	53,497,400 / 100.0%	76 / 100.0%	349	130 / 100.0%

Table A-5

PERCENTAGE OF VOTE, BY LOCAL PREFECTURAL DISTRICT AND PARTY, 1971 AND 1974 HOUSE OF COUNCILLORS ELECTIONS, LOCAL CONSTITUENCIES

District	LDP			JSP			KMT		
	1974	1971	+ −	1974	1971	+ −	1974	1971	+ −
Hokkaido	27.4	48.6	− 21.2	30.8	37.0	− 6.2	14.2	—	—
Aomori	51.0	54.7	− 3.7	24.3	28.5	− 4.2	10.5	—	—
Iwate	47.7	51.9	− 4.2	43.0	39.4	+ 3.6	—	—	—
Miyagi	45.2	40.5	+ 4.7	29.2	44.8	− 15.6	10.5	—	—
Akita	45.7	42.5	+ 3.2	36.8	46.3	− 9.5	—	—	—
Yamagata	53.9	48.0	+ 5.9	32.0	41.2	− 9.2	6.5	—	—
Fukushima	52.1	57.5	− 5.4	33.1	36.3	− 3.2	—	—	—
Ibaragi	24.9	65.7	− 40.8	30.8	28.1	+ 2.7	12.0	—	—
Tochigi	19.6	53.9	− 34.3	25.2	42.1	− 16.9	7.9	—	—
Gumma	52.2	51.9	+ 0.3	31.7	34.1	− 2.4	7.7	—	—
Saitama	42.0	44.3	− 2.3	27.7	39.1	− 11.4	13.4	—	—
Chiba	42.8	42.7	+ 0.1	25.4	32.6	− 7.2	20.0	—	—
Tokyo	23.5	20.0	+ 3.5	20.6	14.5	+ 6.1	15.6	17.5	− 1.9
Kanagawa	25.9	42.7	− 16.8	28.7	37.3	− 8.6	17.9	—	—
Niigata	58.2	48.0	+ 10.2	31.6	42.4	− 10.8	4.9	—	—
Toyama	55.6	56.0	− 0.4	38.5	32.9	+ 5.6	—	—	—
Ishikawa	57.6	59.8	− 2.2	27.9	25.7	+ 2.2	—	—	—
Fukui	60.5	46.5	+ 14.0	30.8	47.1	− 16.3	—	—	—
Yamanashi	42.1	38.7	+ 3.4	41.1	50.5	− 9.4	7.8	—	—
Nagano	41.2	40.4	+ 0.8	34.4	41.8	− 7.4	8.0	—	—
Gifu	51.8	46.1	+ 5.7	23.8	47.5	− 23.7	9.1	—	—
Shizuoka	49.0	59.6	− 10.6	25.8	28.8	− 3.0	9.4	—	—
Aichi	27.7	41.0	− 13.3	18.0	18.9	− 0.9	17.8	—	—
Mie	50.1	53.6	− 3.5	27.0	29.3	− 2.3	12.9	—	—
Shiga	41.2	47.1	− 5.9	29.4	44.8	− 15.4	7.1	—	—
Kyoto	37.2	36.2	+ 1.0	18.6	34.9	− 16.3	14.4	—	—
Osaka	24.0	23.8	+ 0.2	20.0	20.9	− 0.9	22.1	22.5	− 0.4
Hyogo	27.0	48.2	− 21.2	17.7	20.0	− 2.3	19.4	—	—
Nara	52.4	46.5	+ 5.9	22.0	16.7	+ 5.3	13.9	—	—
Wakayama	55.8	65.2	− 9.4	—	19.9	—	23.4	—	—
Tottori	57.4	49.3	+ 8.1	37.9	42.7	− 4.8	—	—	—
Shimane	43.9	37.7	+ 6.2	43.7	39.8	+ 3.9	—	—	—
Okayama	50.9	40.0	+ 10.9	26.4	48.7	− 22.3	16.4	—	—
Hiroshima	53.3	46.5	+ 6.8	27.1	34.7	− 7.6	10.3	—	—
Yamaguchi	49.1	61.5	− 12.4	29.1	28.0	+ 1.1	12.3	—	—
Tokushima	35.3	28.1	+ 7.2	9.0	18.4	− 9.4	6.2	—	—
Kagawa	50.7	44.8	+ 5.9	33.8	50.9	− 17.1	—	—	—
Ehime	46.9	51.3	− 4.4	32.7	33.2	− 0.5	12.0	—	—
Kochi	49.7	33.0	+ 16.7	—	30.4	—	17.3	—	—
Fukuoka	41.0	51.4	− 10.4	25.7	29.8	− 4.1	20.4	—	—
Saga	56.6	70.9	− 14.3	27.6	24.0	+ 3.6	10.1	—	—
Nagasaki	51.9	52.4	− 0.5	28.2	42.6	− 14.4	12.0	—	—
Kumamoto	65.4	66.7	− 1.3	31.2	30.8	+ 0.4	—	—	—
Oita	46.0	42.1	+ 3.9	38.6	52.0	− 13.4	9.0	—	—
Miyazaki	51.0	56.7	− 5.7	29.8	32.4	− 2.6	11.7	—	—
Kagoshima	59.4	53.2	+ 6.2	27.9	27.5	+ 0.4	7.5	—	—
Okinawa	41.1	51.4	− 10.3	—	—	—	—	—	—

Source: Based on statistics from the Ministry of Home Affairs.

	JCP			DSP			MIN			IND		
	1974	1971	+−	1974	1971	+−	1974	1971	+−	1974	1971	+−
	15.7	11.4	+4.3	—	—	—	—	—	—	11.8	3.1	+8.7
	14.1	10.8	+3.3	—	6.0	—	—	—	—	—	—	—
	9.3	8.8	+0.5	—	—	—	—	—	—	—	—	—
	14.0	8.2	+5.8	—	—	—	—	—	—	1.0	6.4	−5.4
	17.5	11.2	+6.3	—	—	—	—	—	—	—	—	—
	7.6	10.8	−3.2	—	—	—	—	—	—	—	—	—
	14.8	6.2	+8.6	—	—	—	—	—	—	—	—	—
	5.7	6.2	−0.5	—	—	—	26.7	—	—	—	—	—
	4.4	3.9	+0.5	6.5	—	—	—	—	—	36.4	—	—
	8.4	8.1	+0.3	—	—	—	—	—	—	—	5.9	—
	15.9	16.5	−0.6	—	—	—	—	—	—	1.1	—	—
	10.7	9.8	+0.9	—	13.1	—	—	—	—	1.2	1.8	−0.6
	15.2	16.2	−1.0	8.3	16.2	−7.9	0.6	0.7	−0.1	16.1	15.0	+1.1
	—	19.9	—	11.8	—	—	—	—	—	15.7	—	—
	5.3	9.6	−4.3	—	—	—	—	—	—	—	—	—
	5.9	6.6	−0.7	—	—	—	—	—	—	—	4.6	—
	14.5	14.5	0.0	—	—	—	—	—	—	—	—	—
	8.7	6.4	+2.3	—	—	—	—	—	—	—	—	—
	6.1	5.9	+0.2	2.9	—	—	—	—	—	—	4.9	—
	16.4	15.2	+1.2	—	—	—	—	—	—	—	2.7	—
	13.3	6.4	+6.9	—	—	—	—	—	—	2.0	—	—
	8.0	10.3	−2.3	6.8	—	—	—	1.2	—	1.1	—	—
	13.2	14.0	−0.8	22.1	18.5	+3.6	—	—	—	1.2	7.6	−6.4
	10.0	17.2	−7.2	—	—	—	—	—	—	—	—	—
	12.9	8.1	+4.8	8.6	—	—	—	—	—	0.7	—	—
	29.3	27.8	+1.5	—	—	—	0.5	—	—	—	1.1	—
	21.8	17.7	+4.1	11.7	14.0	−2.3	—	0.2	—	0.4	0.8	−0.4
	18.4	12.9	+5.5	16.2	18.8	−2.6	—	—	—	1.3	—	—
	11.7	11.7	0.0	—	—	—	—	—	—	—	25.0	—
	20.7	14.9	+5.8	—	—	—	—	—	—	—	—	—
	4.7	5.7	−1.0	—	2.3	—	—	—	—	—	—	—
	5.7	4.7	+1.0	—	—	—	—	—	—	6.7	17.8	−11.1
	6.3	8.4	−2.1	—	—	—	—	3.0	—	—	—	—
	9.2	9.8	−0.6	—	—	—	—	—	—	—	8.9	—
	9.5	10.6	−1.1	—	—	—	—	—	—	—	—	—
	4.5	6.5	−2.0	—	—	—	—	—	—	45.1	47.0	−1.9
	15.5	4.3	+11.2	—	—	—	—	—	—	—	—	—
	7.7	12.6	−4.9	—	—	—	—	—	—	0.7	2.9	−2.2
	33.1	12.2	+20.9	—	—	—	—	—	—	—	24.4	—
	13.0	16.6	−3.6	—	—	—	—	—	—	—	2.1	—
	5.6	5.1	+0.5	—	—	—	—	—	—	—	—	—
	7.9	5.0	+2.9	—	—	—	—	—	—	—	—	—
	3.2	2.5	+0.7	—	—	—	—	—	—	0.2	—	—
	6.4	4.5	+1.9	—	—	—	—	—	—	—	1.4	—
	7.6	11.0	−3.4	—	—	—	—	—	—	—	—	—
	4.0	3.4	+0.6	—	—	—	—	—	—	1.1	15.9	−14.8
	—	—	—	—	—	—	—	—	—	58.9	47.9	+11.0

Table A-6

PERCENTAGE OF VOTE, BY LOCAL PREFECTURAL DISTRICT AND PARTY, 1971 AND 1974 HOUSE OF COUNCILLORS ELECTIONS, NATIONAL CONSTITUENCY

District	LDP 1974	LDP 1971	LDP +−	JSP 1974	JSP 1971	JSP +−	KMT 1974	KMT 1971	KMT +−
Hokkaido	40.8	53.0	− 12.2	24.5	25.5	− 1.0	9.9	10.0	− 0.1
Aomori	54.4	54.5	− 0.1	14.7	18.3	− 3.6	9.6	10.9	− 1.3
Iwate	49.0	45.1	+ 3.9	24.4	33.3	− 8.9	7.3	7.7	− 0.4
Miyagi	49.6	47.1	+ 2.5	17.3	26.6	− 9.3	9.0	11.0	− 2.0
Akita	46.9	48.5	− 1.6	20.5	26.1	− 5.6	9.4	10.4	− 1.0
Yamagata	52.2	53.3	− 1.1	19.7	21.3	− 1.6	7.1	8.7	− 1.6
Fukushima	53.4	47.7	+ 5.7	17.0	22.3	− 5.3	9.6	11.4	− 1.8
Ibaragi	52.9	47.1	+ 5.8	12.7	21.0	− 8.3	12.0	15.4	− 3.4
Tochigi	50.5	49.7	+ 0.8	15.1	19.8	− 4.7	10.5	12.6	− 2.1
Gumma	50.6	49.7	+ 0.9	14.9	18.8	− 3.9	10.8	12.1	− 1.3
Saitama	38.2	36.5	+ 1.7	12.7	22.4	− 9.7	14.1	17.2	− 3.1
Chiba	44.8	40.7	+ 4.1	11.8	22.5	− 10.7	11.9	16.6	− 4.7
Tokyo	34.6	32.6	+ 2.0	10.3	22.3	− 12.0	13.7	16.3	− 2.6
Kanagawa	31.4	28.6	+ 2.8	14.2	23.8	− 9.6	13.0	16.9	− 3.9
Niigata	52.1	49.6	+ 2.5	21.5	25.4	− 3.9	6.5	8.3	− 1.8
Toyama	54.3	56.7	− 2.4	17.0	20.7	− 3.7	5.3	7.6	− 2.3
Ishikawa	55.0	63.9	− 8.9	15.3	17.0	− 1.7	6.7	6.8	− 0.1
Fukui	55.5	58.0	− 2.5	13.4	17.8	− 4.4	7.2	8.7	− 1.5
Yamanashi	50.8	52.3	− 1.5	18.2	18.5	− 0.3	10.6	13.9	− 3.3
Nagano	42.9	44.4	− 1.5	20.6	24.9	− 4.3	9.1	11.7	− 2.6
Gifu	51.1	52.2	− 1.1	14.4	20.6	− 6.2	13.0	11.3	+ 1.7
Shizuoka	52.8	44.9	+ 7.9	11.7	22.1	− 10.4	10.6	14.0	− 3.4
Aichi	41.7	37.9	+ 3.8	12.1	18.4	− 6.3	12.2	14.1	− 1.9
Mie	49.1	49.4	− 0.3	15.0	20.3	− 5.3	10.8	11.8	− 1.0
Shiga	50.1	47.2	+ 2.9	13.4	21.3	− 7.9	6.8	8.1	− 1.3
Kyoto	37.5	34.1	+ 3.4	10.7	19.9	− 9.2	11.3	12.8	− 1.5
Osaka	32.4	31.6	+ 0.8	11.6	21.1	− 9.5	17.7	19.9	− 2.2
Hyogo	38.6	39.3	− 0.7	14.7	21.7	− 7.0	14.8	17.0	− 2.2
Nara	38.1	48.0	− 9.9	13.8	18.3	− 4.5	12.4	17.1	− 4.7
Wakayama	50.2	56.0	− 5.8	11.7	12.7	− 1.0	14.4	16.7	− 2.3
Tottori	52.5	54.4	− 1.9	18.1	19.1	− 1.0	12.9	14.8	− 1.9
Shimane	52.5	51.6	+ 0.9	18.8	20.9	− 2.1	9.6	11.6	− 2.0
Okayama	46.4	47.6	− 1.2	16.1	18.5	− 2.4	13.4	18.4	− 5.0
Hiroshima	50.2	52.2	− 2.0	15.0	16.7	− 1.7	12.9	14.3	− 1.4
Yamaguchi	53.7	55.9	− 2.2	12.7	15.8	− 3.1	12.3	14.4	− 2.1
Tokushima	51.5	57.8	− 6.3	13.0	13.6	− 0.6	15.9	15.7	+ 0.2
Kagawa	50.8	51.8	− 1.0	13.7	21.6	− 7.9	14.9	14.1	+ 0.8
Ehime	51.6	56.8	− 5.2	12.8	14.3	− 1.5	15.2	15.9	− 0.7
Kochi	48.8	51.8	− 3.0	13.7	16.5	− 2.8	14.2	15.5	− 1.3
Fukuoka	39.5	43.1	− 3.6	22.0	21.2	+ 0.8	15.0	18.1	− 3.1
Saga	59.9	63.8	− 3.9	16.8	16.5	+ 0.3	8.5	9.7	− 1.2
Nagasaki	53.4	50.9	+ 2.5	16.7	19.9	− 3.2	10.2	12.6	− 2.4
Kumamoto	59.6	62.3	− 2.7	16.7	17.6	− 0.9	10.5	11.3	− 0.8
Oita	51.9	53.5	− 1.6	22.7	24.1	− 1.4	9.2	11.0	− 1.8
Miyazaki	52.8	54.8	− 2.0	18.3	18.9	− 0.6	9.7	11.7	− 2.0
Kagoshima	60.1	54.3	+ 5.8	17.4	23.8	− 6.4	10.1	11.2	− 1.1
Okinawa	43.0	—	—	17.8	—	—	16.0	—	—

Source: Based on statistics from the Ministry of Home Affairs.

	JCP			DSP			MIN			IND	
1974	1971	+ −	1974	1971	+ −	1974	1971	+ −	1974	1971	+ −
10.2	6.9	+ 3.3	3.7	1.9	+ 1.8	0.2	0.2	0.0	10.7	2.5	+ 8.2
8.2	6.4	+ 1.8	4.4	4.3	+ 0.1	0.1	0.1	0.0	8.6	5.4	+ 3.2
7.2	4.8	+ 2.4	5.4	4.7	+ 0.7	0.1	0.2	− 0.1	6.6	4.2	+ 2.4
8.7	5.4	+ 3.3	5.2	5.0	+ 0.2	0.3	0.2	+ 0.1	9.9	4.7	+ 5.2
10.0	6.5	+ 3.5	4.7	3.9	+ 0.8	0.1	0.4	− 0.3	8.3	4.2	+ 4.1
5.7	5.4	+ 0.3	5.4	5.4	0.0	0.1	0.1	0.0	9.8	5.8	+ 4.0
6.4	5.2	+ 1.2	6.1	5.3	+ 0.8	0.1	0.2	− 0.1	7.5	7.9	− 0.4
5.6	4.4	+ 1.2	3.6	5.3	− 1.7	0.2	0.1	+ 0.1	12.9	6.7	+ 6.2
4.3	3.2	+ 1.1	7.4	8.0	− 0.6	0.1	0.1	0.0	12.1	6.6	+ 5.5
7.5	6.6	+ 0.9	5.1	6.8	− 1.7	0.1	0.3	− 0.2	11.0	5.7	+ 5.3
11.1	8.4	+ 2.7	5.8	7.6	− 1.8	0.1	0.1	0.0	18.0	7.8	+ 10.2
9.3	6.5	+ 2.8	4.9	5.5	− 0.6	0.1	0.1	0.0	17.2	8.0	+ 9.2
12.7	13.2	− 0.5	4.9	5.4	− 0.5	0.1	0.1	0.0	23.7	10.2	+ 13.5
13.0	9.6	+ 3.4	8.8	12.3	− 3.5	0.1	0.1	0.0	19.6	8.7	+ 10.9
6.3	6.1	+ 0.2	6.9	7.1	− 0.2	0.1	0.1	0.0	6.6	3.5	+ 3.1
7.3	4.6	+ 2.7	7.7	6.2	+ 1.5	0.1	0.1	0.0	8.3	4.1	+ 4.2
6.2	4.7	+ 1.5	8.3	5.6	+ 2.7	0.1	0.0	+ 0.1	8.4	2.0	+ 6.4
4.6	3.4	+ 1.2	9.9	7.8	+ 2.1	0.1	0.4	− 0.3	9.3	3.8	+ 5.5
7.2	4.7	+ 2.5	3.5	6.3	− 2.8	0.0	0.0	0.0	9.7	4.3	+ 5.4
13.4	9.3	+ 4.1	5.4	4.4	+ 1.0	0.2	0.1	+ 0.1	8.4	5.2	+ 3.2
6.7	5.1	+ 1.6	5.3	5.4	− 0.1	0.1	0.2	− 0.1	9.4	5.2	+ 4.2
7.0	5.8	+ 1.2	6.9	7.8	− 0.9	0.1	0.1	0.0	10.9	5.3	+ 5.6
9.7	11.1	− 1.4	9.3	11.2	− 1.9	0.2	0.3	− 0.1	14.8	7.1	+ 7.7
6.7	5.8	+ 0.9	6.6	5.8	+ 0.8	0.1	0.2	− 0.1	11.7	6.6	+ 5.1
9.3	7.5	+ 1.8	7.2	9.2	− 2.0	0.2	0.3	− 0.1	13.1	6.4	+ 6.7
21.0	21.5	− 0.5	6.4	6.4	0.0	0.2	0.1	+ 0.1	12.8	5.2	+ 7.6
15.6	15.1	+ 0.5	5.8	6.1	− 0.3	0.1	0.1	0.0	16.8	6.2	+ 10.6
10.8	8.7	+ 2.1	6.4	6.9	− 0.5	0.2	0.1	+ 0.1	14.5	6.4	+ 8.1
7.4	7.0	+ 0.4	15.5	4.8	+ 10.7	0.1	0.1	0.0	12.7	4.8	+ 7.9
10.8	8.5	+ 2.3	4.4	3.1	+ 1.3	0.1	0.0	+ 0.1	8.4	3.0	+ 5.4
4.8	4.7	+ 0.1	3.4	2.7	+ 0.7	0.1	0.1	0.0	8.2	4.3	+ 3.9
5.5	4.3	+ 1.2	6.3	6.2	+ 0.1	0.1	0.1	0.0	7.2	5.2	+ 2.0
6.3	4.6	+ 1.7	6.9	7.2	− 0.3	0.2	0.1	+ 0.1	10.7	3.6	+ 7.1
5.8	4.5	+ 1.3	6.9	8.4	− 1.5	0.2	0.1	+ 0.1	9.0	3.8	+ 5.2
5.9	4.2	+ 1.7	5.7	5.2	+ 0.5	0.1	0.1	0.0	9.6	4.5	+ 5.1
4.2	4.3	− 0.1	4.7	4.3	+ 0.4	0.2	0.1	+ 0.1	10.5	4.2	+ 6.3
5.3	4.0	+ 1.3	5.0	4.4	+ 0.6	0.1	0.0	+ 0.1	10.2	4.0	+ 6.2
5.5	4.5	+ 1.0	5.9	5.7	+ 0.2	0.4	0.0	+ 0.4	8.6	2.8	+ 5.8
12.0	9.9	+ 2.1	3.2	2.6	+ 0.6	0.4	0.1	+ 0.3	7.7	3.6	+ 4.1
9.4	9.4	0.0	4.0	3.8	+ 0.2	0.1	0.1	0.0	10.0	4.3	+ 5.7
3.6	2.8	+ 0.8	4.0	3.4	+ 0.6	0.1	0.1	0.0	7.1	3.7	+ 3.4
4.0	3.4	+ 0.6	7.4	9.1	− 1.7	0.1	0.1	0.0	8.2	4.1	+ 4.1
2.9	2.5	+ 0.4	3.4	2.9	+ 0.5	0.6	0.0	+ 0.6	6.3	3.4	+ 2.9
4.9	4.0	+ 0.9	4.8	4.1	+ 0.7	0.1	0.1	0.0	6.4	3.2	+ 3.2
4.5	3.9	+ 0.6	7.9	5.3	+ 2.6	0.1	0.2	− 0.1	6.7	5.1	+ 1.6
3.4	2.3	+ 1.1	3.6	2.9	+ 0.7	0.1	0.2	− 0.1	5.3	5.2	+ 0.1
13.8	—	—	2.6	—	—	0.1	—	—	6.7	—	—

Table A-7

LDP BUREAUCRATIC-TYPE CANDIDATES: ORGANIZATIONAL SUPPORT, VOTES RECEIVED, AND RANKING, 1974 HOUSE OF COUNCILLORS ELECTION, NATIONAL CONSTITUENCY

Name	Incumbent or New	Major Organizational Support	Votes Received	Rank
Hatoyama Iichirō (Finance Ministry)	New	Tobacco Growers Political League, Sake Brewers Union, PL Kyōdan (religious organization), Sumitomo Group, Dai-ichi Kangyō Bank Group, Nomura Securities, Bridgestone Tire (Hatoyama's father was an LDP prime minister during the mid-fifties.)	1,504,561	4th
Kobayashi Kuniji (Agriculture Ministry)	Incumbent	Construction industry and land development organizations; agricultural cooperatives	867,548	8th
Etō Akira (National Railways)	Incumbent	National Railways, Tenrikyō (religious organization)	701,862	24th
Sakomizu Hisatsune (Finance Ministry)	Incumbent	Tobacco Dealers Association, Bereaved Families Association, Tenrikyō (religious organization), Itō Chū Trading Company, Tōkyū Group (railroad, real estate, department stores)	690,010	25th
Osada Yūji (Ministry of Posts)	Incumbent	Postmasters Association	674,986	29th
Sakano Shigenobu (Construction Ministry)	New	Construction and land development-related industry associations, PL Kyōdan	666,475	31st
Genda Minoru (Self-Defense Forces)	Incumbent	Self-Defense Forces, various organizations of former military men and of several right-wing groups	644,378	37th

144

| Ueda Minoru (Construction Ministry) | Incumbent | Construction industry, real estate associations, Cement Company Association, and other associations related to the building trades | 573,496 | 53rd |
| Okabe Tamotsu [a] (Transportation Ministry) | New | Shipbuilders Association; Warehouse, Dock, and Harbor Association; Ship Captains Association; YKK; Yamaha Engine; transportation-related companies and groups | 511,891 | 61st |

[a] Unsuccessful candidate.

Editor's note: The reader should be aware that a few national-constituency candidates have overlapping backgrounds and sources of political support, a fact which complicates classification. For example, even though Saka Ken and Satō Shinji had had bureaucratic experience, they obtained their major support from outside the bureaucratic structure and therefore are listed in Table A-8. Also, while Curtis classifies Morishita as a business candidate and Genda as an organization-backed candidate, Tomita lists Morishita as organization-backed and Genda as ex-bureaucrat. Such differences, however, are of minor consequence and do not affect the generalizations made in the papers to any significant degree.

Source: *Yomiuri Shimbun*, 12 June 1974.

Table A-8

ORGANIZATION-BACKED LDP CANDIDATES: SUPPORTING ORGANIZATIONS, VOTES RECEIVED AND RANKING, 1974 HOUSE OF COUNCILLORS ELECTION, NATIONAL CONSTITUENCY

Name	Incumbent or New	Major Organizational Support	Votes Received	Rank
Marumo Shigesada [a]	Incumbent	Japan Medical Association	874,662	7th
Satō Shinji [a]	New	Kajima Construction Co., Reiyūkai (religious organization), PL Kyōdan (religious organization), Nihon Kōkan Co., Tokyo Kōgyō Co., Japan Cement Co. (Satō is the son of former Prime Minister Satō.)	718,826	17th
Okada Hiroshi [a]	New	Association of Wartime Pensioners	701,927	23rd
Otani Tōnosuke [a]	Incumbent	Bereaved Families Association	661,332	34th
Morishita Tai [a]	New	Morishita Jintan, Pharmaceutical Association, Suntory, Kansai Electric	573,969	51st
Saka Ken	New	Mitsubishi Group, Police Friends Association, Yuseiren (petroleum interests)	516,159	59th
Maoka Buntarō	New	Japan Dental Association, toothpaste and dental equipment manufacturers, PL Kyōdan	439,015	63rd
Kamei Zenshō	Incumbent	Milk Producers Association, National Fertilizer Council, and organizations associated with forestry, animal husbandry, food, and milling	421,189	66th
Yokoyama Fuku	Incumbent	Japan Midwives Association, Nursing Association, Meiji Milk Co.	365,211	70th
Uchida Yoshirō	Former	LP (liquid propane) gas association, Chamber of Commerce, Yuseiren (petroleum interests)	313,545	71st
Fukushima Tsuneharu	New	Primary, Middle, and High School Principals Association and other educational groups, especially Nikkyōren	308,792	72nd

Note: Satō and Ōtani also had bureaucratic experience.
[a] Successful candidates.
Source: *Yomiuri Shimbun,* 12 June 1974.

Table A-9
MAJOR ORGANIZATIONAL BACKING AND AREA CONCENTRATION OF JSP CANDIDATES, 1974 HOUSE OF COUNCILLORS ELECTION

Name	New or Incumbent	Union Support	Geographical Area
Akune Noboru	Incumbent	Coal, metal miners	Hokkaido, Tochigi, Saitama, Ishikawa, Nagano, Aichi, Nagasaki, Kumamoto
Annō Katsu	New	Postal workers, national railway workers (Shizuoka)	Iwate, Ibaragi, Shizuoka, Ehime, Kochi, Fukuoka, Miyazaki
Kasuya Terumi	New	Nikkyōso (Japan Teachers) for Eastern Japan	Hokkaido, Iwate, Chiba, Tokyo, Kanawaga, Niigata, Yamanashi
Yasunaga Hideo	Incumbent	Nikkyōso (Japan Teachers) for Western Japan	Fukui, Aichi, Okayama, Fukuoka, Oita
Wada Shizuo	Incumbent	Jichirō (local government workers) for Eastern Japan	Gumma, Tokyo, Kanagawa, Niigata, Nagano, Toyama
Noda Tetsu	New	Jichirō (local government workers) for Western Japan, Japan electric industry workers (Hiroshima branch)	Gifu, Mie, Hyogo, Tottori, Shimane, Hiroshima
Katayama Gonichi	New	Telecommunications workers, Agriculture and Forestry Ministry workers	Shiga, Kyoto, Osaka, Wakayama
Matsumoto Eiichi	Incumbent	Buraku Kaihō Dōmei, private railway workers (Kyushu, Kansai regions)	Nara, Yamaguchi, Tokushima, Kagawa, Fukuoka, Saga, Kagoshima, Osaka
Meguro Kesajirō	New	National railways locomotive engineers, Japan Monopoly Corporation workers, printers	Hokkaido, Aomori, Miyagi, Akita, Yamagata, Fukushima
Hata Yutaka	New	Water supply workers, chemical workers, national railway workers (Tokyo, Osaka, Chiba, Okayama)	Saitama, Tokyo, Chiba, Kanagawa, Aichi, Kyoto, Osaka, Hyogo
Katō Shizue [a]	Incumbent	—	Saitama, Tokyo, Kanagawa, Osaka, Hyogo
Tanaka Hajime [a]	Incumbent	Electric machine workers, construction workers	Yamagata, Ibaragi, Tochigi, Saitama, Tokyo, Hyogo

[a] Unsuccessful candidate.

Source: *Yomiuri Shimbun,* 13 June 1974.

Figure A-1

LDP VOTE[a] (IN PERCENTAGE OF TOTAL VOTE),
HOUSE OF REPRESENTATIVES AND
HOUSE OF COUNCILLORS ELECTIONS, 1959–1974

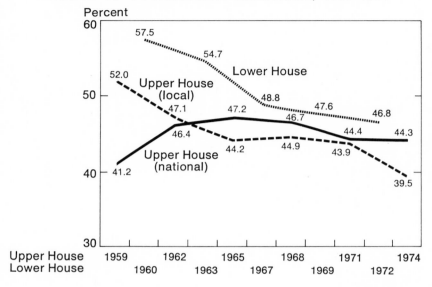

[a] Excludes conservative-related independent candidates, some of whom joined the LDP following the election.

Source: Ministry of Home Affairs data.

Figure A-2

CHANGING VOTING RATES OF MEN AND WOMEN,
HOUSE OF COUNCILLORS ELECTIONS, 1947–1974

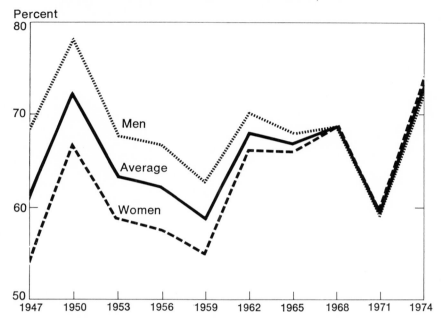

Source: Ministry of Home Affairs data.

CONTRIBUTORS

MICHAEL BLAKER, until recently, directed the Japanese policy studies program sponsored by the United Nations Association. A specialist on Japanese domestic politics and foreign relations, Dr. Blaker is currently a research associate at the East Asian Institute at Columbia University. His scholarly studies include a monograph on Japanese international bargaining behavior before World War II and essays on Japanese diplomacy, foreign policy decision-making processes, and U.S.-Japanese security relations.

GERALD L. CURTIS is associate professor of political science and director of the East Asian Institute at Columbia University. He is the author of *Election Campaigning Japanese Style,* the Japanese edition of which is now in its fourteenth printing, and editor of *Japanese-American Relations in the 1970's.* He has published widely in both Japanese and English on topics relating to contemporary Japanese domestic politics and U.S.-Japanese affairs.

HERBERT PASSIN is chairman of the Department of Sociology at Columbia University and a member of the university's East Asian Institute. He has lived in Japan for many years, and he has written extensively on his researches there. His books include *The Japanese Village in Transition* (with Arthur F. Raper and others, 1951), *In Search of Identity* (with John W. Bennett, 1958), *Society and Education in Japan* (1965), and *The United States and Japan* (editor, 1975).

NOBUO TOMITA is professor of political science and director of the faculty of political science at Meiji University in Tokyo. Among his many works are *Gendai seiji to gikaisei minshushugi* [Contemporary politics and parliamentary democracy] and *Hoshu dokusai no teihen: gendai Nihon no seiji ishiki* [Modern Japanese political consciousness: a foundation of conservative rule], of which he is coauthor, and numerous articles on political subjects for mass circulation magazines and scholarly journals, including articles on political attitudes, party politics, and electoral behavior.

INDEX

153

Cover and book design: Pat Taylor